August 27, 2013

Happy Anniversary♡

Love you, Anne

À LA GRECQUE

our Greek table

First published in 2009 by Hardie Grant Books
This edition published in 2013 by Hardie Grant Books

An SBS book

Hardie Grant Books (Australia)
Ground Floor, Building 1
658 Church Street
Richmond, Victoria 3121
www.hardiegrant.com.au

Hardie Grant Books (UK)
Dudley House, North Suite
34–35 Southampton Street
London WC2E 7HF
www.hardiegrant.co.uk

Cataloguing-in-Publication data is available from the
National Library of Australia.

ISBN 978 1 7427 0486 9

Edited by Lucy Rushbrooke
Art direction and design by Gayna Murphy, Greendot Design
Cover design by Heather Menzies
Photography by Mark Roper and Robert Ashton
Styling by Leesa O'Reilly
Colour reproduction by Splitting Image Colour Studio
Printed and bound in China by 1010 Printing International Limited

10 9 8 7 6 5 4 3 2 1

The publisher would like to thank the following for their generosity in
supplying props for the book: A Day on Earth, The Essential Ingredient,
Greg Hatton, Hub, Izzi & Popo, Manon Bis, Moss Melbourne, North Carlton
Ceramics and Seneca Textiles.

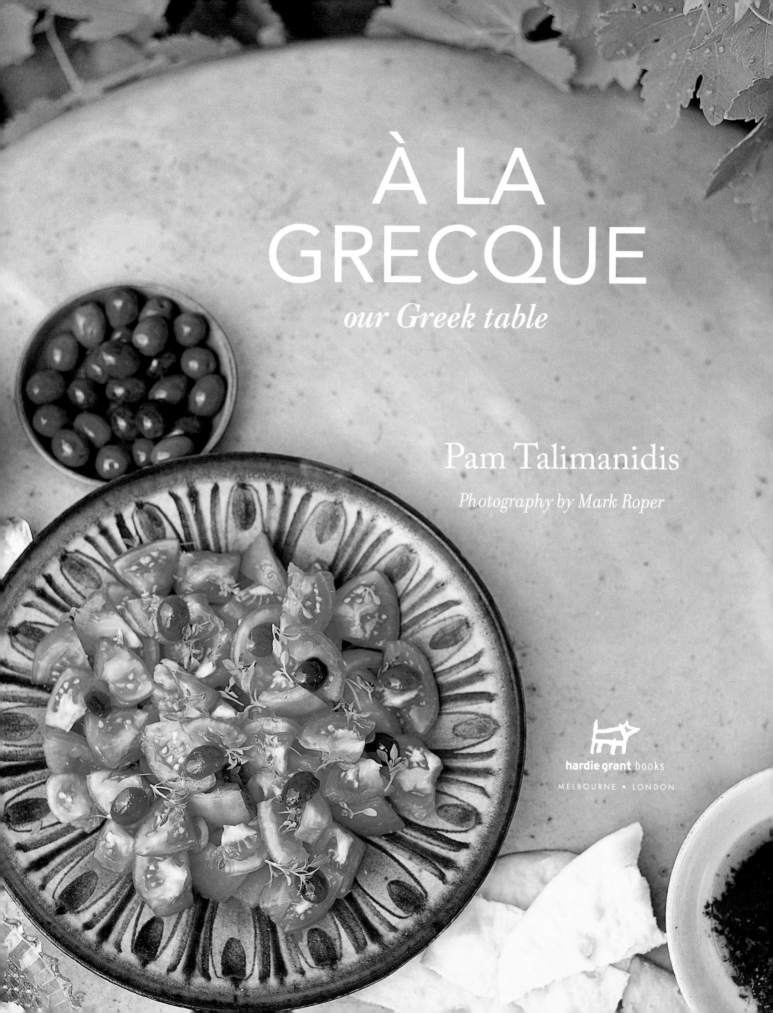

À LA GRECQUE

our Greek table

Pam Talimanidis

Photography by Mark Roper

hardie grant books

MELBOURNE • LONDON

Contents

Gift

A day so happy.
Fog lifted early. I worked in the garden.
Hummingbirds were stopping over the honeysuckle flowers.
There was no thing on earth I wanted to possess.
I knew no one worth my envying him.
Whatever evil I had suffered, I forgot.
To think that once I was the same man did not embarrass me.
In my body I felt no pain.
When straightening up, I saw blue sea and sails.

(Czeslaw Milosz, 1911–2004)

In memory of my mother-in-law,
who embraced me as a foreign daughter in-law
and loved me like a daughter.

Introduction

I had seen the premises of A la Grecque in Aireys Inlet many times. It had been built as a restaurant and had changed hands and names repeatedly. It had always seemed to me rather sad, a place you just drove past. When my husband Kosta told me it was for sale and asked me to look at it, I couldn't see anything to like about it. Three times I said no. But, being Kosta, he bought it anyway. That was in 2004.

I met Kosta in 1977 while I was still at university. He had only just opened his restaurant in Lorne, which was then called The Steak Place. Being in love with a mad Greek distracted me from my studies but, somewhat miraculously, I passed my law degree and moved to the coast with Kosta. Lorne was then a small village and we were friends with the other shopkeepers in the main street. We partied all night and swam all day and in between managed to run the restaurant. Gradually, however, we began to take the business more seriously. We renamed it Kostas Taverna and from there, 'Kostas' took on its own identity. It developed into an iconic eating place on the Great Ocean Road, renowned for its great atmosphere – largely a result of Kosta's sense of fun – and its simple, fresh food. We added dishes to the menu, some experimental, some traditional; fresh fish and seafood were mainstays, along with Greek flavours, oils and spices.

Thankfully, after we married and had children, Kosta's parents came to Australia to help us care for our sons, Alex, Stratos and Dominic. My mother-in-law, Kyria Domna, was endlessly patient with me, carefully teaching me Greece's beautiful language and its cooking. She showed me the importance of thoughtful preparation, being sure to avoid wasting precious ingredients.

After we had been in the restaurant industry for nearly thirty years at Kostas Taverna, what had once been fun and challenging became less so. I began to feel that being in the same place for so long was smothering us. Customers had started to dictate their expectations, protesting when anything changed and stifling creativity in the kitchen. We sold Kostas in 2003 and for a year played in the garden, went camping and spent time with our boys.

Opening A la Grecque breathed new life into us. The uncertainty of starting a new business, and in a town previously unable to sustain a restaurant, kept us on our toes. There were no guarantees. We were apprehensive, but we knew the direction we wanted to take and felt invigorated by the prospect. We knocked off all the extra bits and pieces that had been added onto the building over the years — closed verandahs, tool sheds, fences, windmills — to reveal the original structure. A new kitchen, some fresh paint, a cycle of frescoes by our friend Domenico de Clario, new furniture, new menu and we were in business with a fresh canvas.

Simplicity. That was to be our mantra. Seasonal, fresh, simple. Just the kind of food we ate at home. A family restaurant, where it was a great experience not only for the customers but also for us.

Running a restaurant in a small seaside town on the south-west coast of Victoria, primarily a summer holiday destination, meant that we worked very hard in the summer but the winter months were quiet. So each year we took off to Kosta's village, Polypetron, in the north of Greece for a long holiday over June and July. We still do it. The boys missed school in their younger years but learnt in other ways, in particular, the history and culture of their ancestry, speaking fluent Greek, getting to know their cousins and grandparents and understanding the workings of a small Greek agricultural village.

Polypetron has become a second home to me. When we are there we live the local life. We go to the daily markets in nearby villages and our whole day revolves around planning dinner. We grow as much as we can in the garden. The excellent soil and warm climate mean that soon after we arrive we can harvest produce from our own garden. In the interim, friends and neighbours offer whatever produce they have, so that we are never without fresh vegetables and eggs. Our cherry trees are laden with fruit at the end of spring, followed shortly by apricots, peaches and plums and, just as we are leaving, the figs and grapes begin to ripen.

In the village we relax completely in the familiar company of relatives and long-time friends. We read, take a siesta in the afternoon, drink our coffee under the branches of a massive walnut tree and walk to the next village, where we greet old friends along the way.

....

What I most admire about Greek family life is that the families stay together and look after one another. Many households accommodate three or more generations; grandparents look after grandchildren, especially for the long summer holiday. Keeping our family together while running a restaurant, with both of us working nights, was not always easy. I insisted on the family sitting down to meals together, at least for breakfast and lunch, and at night the boys often worked in the restaurant with us. When they were teenagers they disappeared whenever they saw an opportunity, but Kosta would find them and drag them back to work. Now they have all grown up to be excellent workers. Alex joined us as a partner in the business and is now with me in the kitchen as our number-one chef. All of our sons were proficient in the kitchen at an early age; peeling carrots and garlic, and shelling peas and broad (fava) beans were second nature to them. Everyone pitched in. Through it all, we know we can rely on one another regardless of the difficulties.

The phrase 'à la grecque' – 'in the Greek way' – perfectly conveys the style of food I had in mind when we started our new restaurant. The expression gave me the license to interpret Greek cooking to include the influences of surrounding Mediterranean countries – European and Middle Eastern – while making use of the amazing produce of Australia, and the best condiments and produce of Greece that are so readily available here.

The Greek table is a place of sharing. It reflects the yearly cycle of the garden and the foods that are unique to each season, the careful and loving preparation of fresh produce, and, most importantly, the offering of 'filoxenia' – friendship and hospitality. In the recipes that follow I hope to share with you the joys of an abundant Greek table and to show you how preparing and eating good food are the essentials of wellbeing.

....

Yiayia

Kyria Domna, Kosta's mother, was a vibrant, intelligent and capable woman. She was born in 1912, in a small Turkish village called Kiz Dervent (meaning girl-in-the-guesthouse) on the silk route south of Istanbul. She became a refugee at the age of ten when Kemal Attaturk introduced his infamous series of population exchanges. As a result of this controversial decision, Orthodox Christians, who had co-existed happily with their Muslim neighbours for centuries in Turkey, were uprooted from their family homes and 'repatriated' to Greece, while Muslim families from Greece were re-settled in Turkey.

In 1922, both Kosta's mother (Yiayia) and his father Strato (Papou) were forced to flee from Turkey with their extended families to a displaced persons' camp in northeastern Greece, before eventually being re-settled by the Greek government in the small village of Polypetron, 50 kilometres (30 miles) northwest of Thessaloniki. To this day, the village is roughly divided into two halves: the Trakatrurki, whose families were refugees, and the original local inhabitants, the Endopia, who are of Slavic extraction. They co-exist peacefully, and these days intermarrying is becoming more common, but the two different races are easy to pick, defined by hair and skin colouring, as well as their food, language and habits.

Life for refugee families such as Yiayia's was very hard. Having left their homes and belongings back in Turkey, they had to start again with nothing in a new country in a time of great privation. Over the course of Yiayia's childhood years she experienced war, poverty and hunger. Her parents farmed a couple of acres where they grew sesame seeds, wheat and as many vegetables as they could. Transport was by donkey and crops were harvested by hand. Domna was an extremely bright girl and wanted to be a teacher, but her brothers opposed this idea. Instead she was married against her will at the age of sixteen and bore six children.

In the home where she raised her family there was no electricity and water had to be carried by hand from a nearby well. Water for bathing and washing clothes was heated in an olive oil tin over a makeshift wood fire outside in the yard. Ash from the fire was used to scrub the dirt off work-clothes and the children were bathed once a week on Saturdays, to be clean for church on Sunday.

I first met Yiayia in 1977 when I followed Kosta to his village in Greece. I was young and in love and very anxious about how I would be received by his family. In those days arranged marriages were still the norm and Greek families certainly did not invite their sons' girlfriends to stay. Luckily for me, I was welcomed warmly and made to feel at home. I spoke not a word of Greek, but as Yiayia was endlessly patient and persistent I was soon able to communicate and perform some tasks to her satisfaction. I realised from the moment I met Yiayia that she would be a key part of my life with Kosta, and I was determined to please her and to be accepted.

....

Although I had come from a large family and was raised on a farm, I had grown up with the usual modern conveniences and was quite unused to washing clothes by hand, sweeping the whole house with a straw broom, shaking carpets and blankets daily and having a bath in a bucket. At first Yiayia would inspect everything I did, and more often than not I was chided and corrected, so that tasks were completed strictly in line with recognised standards of village protocol. I did find this rather hard to take and many times I complained bitterly to Kosta about Yiayia's bossiness and criticism. But I grew to love her dearly and came to respect the traditions which she upheld.

Over the next few decades Yiayia became a huge influence on my life, especially in the kitchen. It was she who taught me to cook and she is the reason that I cook in our restaurant today. She herself was a proud and accomplished cook, and preparing food was a responsibility that she embraced with passion and precision. She planned every meal of the week in advance, doing the preparation slowly and meticulously. Every meal was then critically analysed and dissected at the table: flavours and balance, cooking times and procedure were all discussed – near enough was not good enough.

The first lesson I learnt from Yiayia was that nothing in the kitchen is wasted. Winters in northern Greece are harsh and long, with little fresh food available, so families rely heavily on their own food reserves. During the summer months, excess vegetables and fruit from the garden are preserved for the winter months. Onions, garlic and potatoes are carefully stored in a cool, dark place. Tomatoes, apricots and plums are dried in the hot sun or made into sauces and jams. Beans and peas are dried for soups and stews. Grapes are crushed to make ouzo and wine vinegar. Milk is made into feta cheese, which is stored in brine for the months ahead. Excess eggs are used to make 'trakhana', a fine pasta that is cooked like porridge and served with honey or with crumbled feta.

The most precious ingredient of all is olive oil, which in Yiayia's kitchen was always measured out carefully and precisely. Whenever I thought the tin was empty, Yiayia would rest it upside down in a bowl out in the sun to drain out every last drop.

Soups

Bean soups, particularly fassolatha and fakes, are a staple of the Greek diet. They are consumed regularly, not as a first course but as a whole meal. There are three reasons for this: they make a substantial meal on the many days of religious fasting when eating meat is prohibited; they are very nutritious, being high in protein, fibre and carbohydrate; they are inexpensive to make. With the addition of olive oil and vegetables and accompanied by a number of simple side dishes and some crusty bread, these soups are filling and tasty and are consumed all year round.

Greeks are great fish eaters and never like to waste anything edible, so housewives will often make a stock from the head of a fish to make a simple psarosoupa. Sometimes this basic stock will be made into a more complex kakavia, with the addition of potato and other seafood.

The celebration of Easter is the most important religious festival in the Greek calendar and the preparation of the spring lamb for the spit on Easter Sunday is eagerly anticipated. But before the feasting comes maygeritsa, a soup made from the lamb offal (variety meat) that is served after midnight mass to officially break the Lenten fasting. Avgolemono (egg and lemon) is whisked into the soup just before serving.

A special treat for late night revellers is a tripe soup called patsa, which is consumed on the way home from the bouzoukia (night clubs), usually at around 3 or 4 am. Special patsa shops stay open all night to cater for this trade, fortifying those who will go straight to work with little or no sleep but a satisfied stomach. Patsa is also consumed by early morning shift workers on their way to work.

Chicken stock

This chicken stock can be used for many dishes
Keep some in the freezer for handy use.

When I make this stock at home, I will often
rub the cooked chicken with salt and olive oil
after I remove it from the stock, then roast it
in a hot oven with the top element on, for about
fifteen minutes, to brown it quickly. It makes a
wonderful easy lunch or dinner, served with
anchovy mayonnaise, a crisp lettuce salad and
fresh bread.

2 onions
2 carrots
2 stalks celery
2 leeks
6 stalks parsley
3 cloves garlic
6 whole black peppercorns
2 litres (68 fl oz) water
1 large free-range chicken
salt

Wash all the vegetables and herbs thoroughly.
Chop the vegetables and garlic roughly then put
them into a stockpot or large saucepan with the
parsley and peppercorns. Cover with the water
and bring to the boil, then lower the heat and
simmer for 1 hour.

Rinse the chicken well and pat dry with kitchen
paper. Lower it into the vegetable stock and
return to a gentle boil. Simmer for 45 minutes,
uncovered, skimming away any impurities that
rise to the surface.

Lift the chicken onto a plate and set aside for
dinner or another use. Strain the stock through
a colander then taste and season with salt to your
liking. If not using straight away, when the stock
is completely cold, divide it into batches and
refrigerate or freeze.

Makes about 1.5 litres (51 fl oz)

Lamb stock

2 onions
2 carrots
2 stalks celery
6 stalks parsley
3 cloves garlic
2 lamb necks or lamb shanks
6 whole black peppercorns
2 litres (68 fl oz) water

Preheat the oven to 180°C (350°F).

Wash all the vegetables and herbs thoroughly.
Chop the vegetables and garlic roughly and place
them on a baking tray with the lamb necks or
shanks. Roast for 1–1½ hours until both meat and
vegetables are brown and crisp.

Tip everything into a stockpot or large saucepan.
Add the parsley, peppercorns and water and
bring to the boil. Lower the heat and simmer for
1½–2 hours, uncovered, skimming away any
impurities that rise to the surface.

Strain the stock through a colander, discarding
the solids and leave it to cool. Once cold,
refrigerate overnight. The fat will set into a solid
layer on the surface and can be easily lifted off.
If not using straight away, divide the stock into
batches and refrigerate or freeze.

Makes about 1.5 litres (51 fl oz)

Fish stock

In my view, the secret to making fish stock is to make the vegetable stock first and add the fish later. It only needs to be simmered for about twenty minutes to extract all the flavour from the fish and keeps a touch of sweetness in the stock. Use the stock for soups and casseroles and for cooking seafood rice dishes.

Use whatever pieces of fish you like: the head and fins from a large snapper and flathead off-cuts are all ideal.

....

2 onions
2 carrots
1 stalk celery
1 leek
6 stalks parsley
3 sprigs thyme
2 litres (68 fl oz) water
700 g (1 lb 9 oz) fish pieces, scaled and
    well rinsed
10 whole black peppercorns

Wash all the vegetables and herbs thoroughly. Chop the vegetables roughly then put them into a stockpot or large saucepan with the parsley and thyme. Cover with water and bring to the boil, then lower the heat and simmer for 40 minutes.

Add the fish pieces and return the stock to a gentle boil. Simmer for 20 minutes, uncovered. Skim the stock if any impurities rise to the surface.

Strain the stock through a colander, discarding the solids, then taste and season with salt and pepper to your liking. If not using straight away, when the stock is completely cold, divide it into batches and refrigerate or freeze.

Makes about 1.5 litres (51 fl oz)

Chicken, green pea and kritharaki soup

This very simple soup relies on using a full-flavoured home-made chicken stock, such as the one opposite. Kritharaki is a small rice-shaped pasta, similar to risoni. The soup can also be made with rice, instead of pasta, but you need to wash the rice well and to pre-cook it before adding it to the stock, to prevent the soup from turning cloudy.

....

1.5 litres (51 fl oz) Chicken Stock (opposite)
160 g (5 ⅔ oz) kritharaki or risoni pasta
300 g (10 ½ oz) fresh peas (shelled weight) or
    good quality frozen peas
salt
freshly ground black pepper

In a large saucepan, bring the stock to a boil. Add the kritharaki slowly, stirring all the time. Boil for 10 minutes then add the peas. Simmer gently for a further 5 minutes or until the peas are tender. Season with salt and pepper to taste.

Serves 4

Greek fish soup Psarosoupa

My mother-in-law, Yiayia, could never believe that Australians would waste the head of a fish. To her it was a delicacy and the meat in the cheek cavities was prized for being especially soft, silky and sweet. She would make soup for the whole family whenever she could procure a snapper head. From her I learned that the secret to a great fish soup is in making a vegetable stock first, then adding the fish head and only cooking it for twenty minutes. This way the flavour from the fish is imparted and the flesh stays moist and delicious.

You can also use this recipe to make a basic fish stock. Just strain and discard the vegetables and fish and keep the liquid for a stock.

1 large snapper head
salt
2 carrots, diced
2 stalks celery, diced
2 onions, diced
2 potatoes, diced

1 leek, sliced and well washed
2 cloves garlic, finely chopped
4 stalks parsley
180 ml (6 fl oz) olive oil
freshly ground black pepper
juice of 1 lemon

Wash the snapper head well. Make sure that the gills have been completely removed and that there is no blood remaining in the spinal cavity. Sprinkle lightly with salt and set aside.

Place the vegetables, garlic and parsley in a saucepan that is large enough to fit the whole snapper head. Cover generously with cold water and bring to the boil. Reduce the heat and simmer for about 40 minutes until the potato and carrot are nearly cooked.

Increase the heat and add the olive oil to the pan. Boil rapidly for about 5 minutes, so that soup becomes milky and opaque. Lift some of the vegetables out of the stock and transfer them to a large soup tureen or individual serving bowls.

Add the snapper head to the saucepan. Bring to the boil then lower the heat and simmer for 20 minutes.

Lift the snapper head out of the soup and place it on a large platter. Pick out the meat from the cheek cavities and add it to the vegetables in the tureen or distribute it among the individual bowls.

Season the soup with pepper and add lemon juice to taste. You may strain it if you wish as sometimes there are a few scales left behind. Pour the hot soup over the vegetables and fish and serve immediately.

Serves 6

Lentil soup Fakes

Although they are often underrated, lentils have a high protein and iron content and make one of my favourite soups. Fakes must be creamy, not watery, so be generous with the olive oil. It is also important to boil the soup rapidly after you add the oil so that it emulsifies the liquid. Add a spoonful of good quality wine vinegar to serve and taste the way the sharpness of the vinegar lifts the flavour of the soup.

Any leftover fakes can be stirred through a simple rice pilaf, and topped with fried onions to make a delicious lunch.

250 g (9 oz) Puy lentils, washed and drained
1.3 litres (44 fl oz) water
1 small onion, diced
1 carrot, diced
1 stalk celery, diced
2 cloves garlic, chopped
1 potato, cubed (optional)

1 teaspoon ground cumin
salt
freshly ground black pepper
190 ml (6 ½ fl oz) olive oil
1 large handful spinach leaves, washed (optional)
a splash of good quality white wine vinegar
olives, feta and crusty bread to serve

Place the lentils in a heavy-based saucepan and cover with the water. Add the onion, carrot, celery, garlic and potato, if using. Bring to the boil then reduce the heat and simmer gently for 1 hour, or until the lentils and vegetables are soft. The lentils should still retain their form and be soft but not mushy.

Add the cumin, salt, pepper and oil. Boil vigorously for about 5 minutes, so that the oil emulsifies and thickens the soup. It should be fairly liquid, not a thick sludgy mass, so you may need to add a little more water.

When ready to serve, add the spinach, if using, and stir until it wilts into the hot soup. Serve with a splash of vinegar, olives, feta and crusty bread.

Serves 4

Smoked cod, salmon and potato soup

This is not strictly a Greek recipe, but rather, a variation of a Scottish fish soup. It is thick and chunky and the flavours are intense and satisfying. We often serve this soup at A la Grecque and it's always popular.

1 kg (2 lb 3 oz) smoked cod fillets
750 ml (25 fl oz) milk
300 g (10 ½ oz) butter
2 onions, finely chopped
4 large potatoes, chopped
2 litres (68 fl oz) Fish Stock (page 27)

1 cup chopped parsley
250 g (9 oz) smoked salmon, finely chopped
1 bay leaf
½ teaspoon salt
½ teaspoon freshly ground black pepper
cream to serve

Place the smoked cod fillets and milk in a heavy-based saucepan. Bring the milk to a gentle simmer and poach gently, without allowing it to boil, until the fish is soft.

Remove the pan from the heat and when the fish is cool enough to handle, strain off and reserve the milk. Flake the fish, removing and discarding the bones and skin.

Melt the butter in a large saucepan and sauté the onions until soft and translucent. Add all the remaining ingredients, except for the cream, and simmer for about 20 minutes, until the potatoes are beginning to disintegrate. Add the reserved milk and flaked fish to the pan and simmer for another minute or so, just to warm them through. Adjust the seasoning to your taste, then ladle into soup bowls and drizzle a little cream on top to serve.

Serves 8

Mussel, tomato and basil soup

Whenever possible, for reasons of freshness, I like to use locally caught mussels. I ask my fishmonger to let me know when they have a delivery of good-sized mussels so I know I'll be getting optimum quality.

120 ml (4 fl oz) olive oil
2 onions, diced
2 cloves garlic, chopped
6 ripe tomatoes, skinned and diced
1 litre (34 fl oz) Fish Stock (page 27)
500 g (1 lb 2 oz) mussels, scrubbed clean and
    beards removed

150 ml (5 fl oz) white wine
½ cup basil, chopped
60 ml (2 fl oz) Pernod
freshly ground black pepper
basil oil or chilli oil (optional) to serve

Heat the olive oil in a deep saucepan and sauté the onions until soft and translucent. Add the garlic and cook until golden. Add the tomatoes and cook for a few minutes until they begin to soften. Add the fish stock and bring to the boil. Simmer for a few minutes.

Meanwhile, put the mussels and white wine into another large saucepan with a tight-fitting lid. Cook over a low–medium heat, shaking the pan gently from time to time. Check after 4 minutes and discard any mussels that haven't opened. Tip into a colander and reserve the cooking liquid. Strain this liquid through a clean piece of muslin (cheesecloth) to remove any sand or grit.

Set aside about a quarter of the mussels to serve in their shells as garnish. Remove the mussel meat from the remaining shells and add to the simmering soup. Add the basil and Pernod and season with pepper. Taste the soup before adding some of the reserved mussel cooking liquid. You want the mussel flavour, but it can be very salty.

Simmer the soup gently for a few minutes, but do not allow it to boil, as the mussels will shrink and become tough and rubbery. Divide the reserved mussels in their shells among 6 soup bowls and pour the soup over them. Drizzle with a little basil oil or chilli oil (if using) and serve straight away.

Serves 6

Greek bean soup Fassolatha

This soup is a classic staple in the Greek diet, both in summer and winter. The beans are grown during the summer, and collected and dried in the sun to last through winter. In the summer fassolatha is eaten at room temperature, and served with salty side dishes such as ranga (smoked and dried mackerel), anchovies, olives or feta and a few spring onions (scallions) for crunch. In the winter, a steaming bowl of fassolatha with fresh crusty bread warms one from the inside. This soup is a meal in itself, it is not intended to be served as a starter.

600 g (1 lb 5 oz) dried cannellini beans
1 onion, diced
1 carrot, diced
1 stalk celery, diced
2 cloves garlic, sliced

1 teaspoon salt
½ teaspoon freshly ground black pepper
½ cup roughly chopped flat-leaf (Italian) parsley
1 tablespoon tomato paste (concentrated purée)
190 ml (6 ½ fl oz) olive oil

Wash the beans to remove any dust or little stones. Cover generously with cold water and soak overnight. The next day, drain the beans and tip them into a large saucepan with the onion, carrot, celery and garlic. Cover generously with fresh cold water and bring to the boil. Simmer for about 1 hour, or until the beans can be easily squashed between your thumb and forefinger.

Add the salt, pepper and parsley to the saucepan. Dissolve the tomato paste in a little of the hot liquid, then stir into the soup. Add the olive oil and bring to the boil. Boil vigorously for a few minutes, so that the soup becomes thick and creamy. Serve in deep bowls with your choice of suggested accompaniments, depending on the season.

Serves 6

Roasted tomato and red capsicum soup with dukkah

The flavour and sweetness of the tomatoes are intensified by roasting them. As some of the liquid evaporates, they will caramelise and the olive oil and salt and pepper will enhance the richness of the tomato flavour.

The dukkah recipe makes about 500 g (1 lb 2 oz), but is well worth making in large amounts. It will keep in an airtight container for a month or more and is also delicious served with crusty bread and extra virgin olive oil as a start to a meal, or sprinkled on eggs for breakfast.

....

Soup
1 kg (2 lb 3 oz) ripe tomatoes
4 red capsicums (peppers)
1 long green chilli
salt
freshly ground black pepper
120 ml (4 fl oz) olive oil
2 onions, diced
2 cloves garlic, chopped
2 teaspoons sugar (optional, depending on the
    sweetness of the tomatoes)
300 ml (10 fl oz) verjuice

6 slices sourdough baguette
3 tablespoons olive oil
100 g (3 ½ oz) feta

Dukkah
250 g (9 oz) raw almonds
150 g (5 oz) sesame seeds
1 tablespoon cumin seeds
1 tablespoon coriander seeds
1 tablespoon fennel seeds
1 teaspoon whole white peppercorns
1 teaspoon salt

To make the dukkah, preheat the oven to 180°C (350°F) then roast each ingredient on separate baking trays until fragrant and lightly coloured. Be careful not to overcook the spices as they will become bitter.

Pound separately using a mortar and pestle or a spice grinder until all are finely ground. Mix all the ingredients together and store in an airtight container.

To make the soup, preheat the oven to 180°C (350°F) and lightly oil 2 baking trays.

Cut the tomatoes in half horizontally and place them on a baking tray, cut side up. Place the capsicums and chilli on the other tray. Sprinkle everything generously with salt and pepper and drizzle on half the olive oil.

Roast the capsicums and chilli for about 40 minutes, until soft. Transfer to a bowl and cover with plastic wrap. When cool enough to handle, peel the capsicums and chilli and remove the seeds. Roast the tomatoes for 45 minutes, or until soft and beginning to colour. Remove from the oven.

Heat the remaining oil in a large saucepan and sauté the onions until soft and golden. Add the garlic, followed by the roasted tomatoes, capsicums and chilli. Stir everything together, then add the sugar and verjuice. Bring to the boil then lower the heat and simmer for 20 minutes. The soup should be fairly liquid and you may need to add a little water.

Allow the soup to cool a little then blend in a food processor. For a really smooth finish, push the soup through a chinois or a very fine sieve. Taste and adjust the seasoning to your liking.

....

When ready to serve, brush the sourdough bread slices with olive oil and bake in a medium oven until golden brown. Spread each slice with feta and sprinkle generously with dukkah, pushing it into the cheese so it stays there.

Reheat the soup (if necessary) and ladle into serving bowls. Float a slice on top of the soup and serve straight away.

Serves 6

Zucchini and red capsicum soup

At the end of the summer when you have an abundance of zucchinis (courgettes) in the garden and you're struggling to think of new ways to use them up, try this soup for a light lunch. Add a bullet chilli if you want to spice it up a bit, or try crumbling on feta cheese or drizzling with basil oil just before serving.

2 small red capsicums (peppers)
120 ml (4 fl oz) extra virgin olive oil
1 small onion, diced
2 cloves garlic, chopped
4 small–medium zucchinis (courgettes), roughly chopped

1 litre (34 fl oz) Chicken Stock (page 26), or water if you want a vegetarian soup
salt
freshly ground black pepper

Preheat the oven to 200°C (400°F) and lightly oil a small baking tray.

Arrange the capsicums on the baking tray and brush with a little oil. Roast for 30 minutes, or until the skins are blistered and the capsicums are soft. Transfer the capsicums to a bowl and cover with plastic wrap. When they are cool enough to handle, peel off the skin and cut them in half. Slice away the seeds and white membranes. Roughly chop 3 of the capsicum halves and slice the remaining piece into strips to use as garnish.

Heat the remaining olive oil in a heavy-based saucepan. Sauté the onion and garlic over a low–medium heat until soft and transparent. Add the chopped capsicum and fry with the onion and garlic for a few minutes. Add the zucchini and stir in well. Add the stock and seasonings and bring to the boil. Lower the heat and simmer for 15–20 minutes until all the vegetables are tender.

Tip into a food processor and purée to a smooth consistency. Serve garnished with the reserved strips of roasted capsicum.

Serves 4

Lamb broth with green garlic

This is a hearty soup for a cold spring day. Green garlic is young garlic with green leaves that has just formed a head. It can be tricky to source, but your greengrocer should be able to get it if you order it ahead of time. The best way to secure a supply of green garlic is to grow your own, simply by planting garlic cloves that have a green shoot in them. You can do this all year round, but especially in autumn and winter. Pull them up in the spring when the bulb has formed under the ground but is still green and not dried.

750 g (1 lb 10 oz) lamb leg meat
1 teaspoon salt
1 teaspoon freshly ground black pepper
120 ml (4 fl oz) extra virgin olive oil
3 onions, sliced

3 potatoes, diced
1½ litres (51 fl oz) Lamb Stock (page 26)
4 stalks green garlic, washed and cut into
   3 cm (1¾ in) lengths

Trim off as much fat as you can from the lamb and cut into 2.5 cm (1 in) cubes. Season with salt and pepper.

Heat some of the oil in a large, heavy-based saucepan. Brown the meat in batches, until it is well coloured all over. It is important not to overcrowd the pan or the lamb will boil, rather than fry, and will not colour. Transfer the browned meat to a bowl.

When all the lamb has been browned, add a little more oil to the pan and sauté the onions until soft and golden. Add the potatoes and stir so that everything is coated with the oil. Return the meat to the pan and add the lamb stock.

Heat a little more olive oil in a small saucepan and wilt the garlic until soft. Reserve some for garnish and add the rest to the soup. Bring to the boil, then lower the heat and simmer for 2 hours. The meat should be very tender and the potatoes should break up and thicken the liquid.

Taste and adjust the seasoning to your liking. Ladle into bowls and serve garnished with the reserved garlic.

Serves 6

A Greek wedding

Kosta and I were married in the month of June at Moni Vlatathon, a monastery set in the ancient castle wall above Thessaloniki where peacocks roamed the grounds – the same monastery where St Paul addressed the Thessalonians, two thousand years earlier.

Being married in Greece was an exotic and romantic dream, but obtaining permission from the higher powers of the Greek Orthodox Church proved to be more difficult than Kosta and I had imagined. We travelled the highways, going from the local priest, to the bishop, to the primate, trying to obtain the necessary papers. We drew up legal documents binding our future children to the Greek Orthodox Church, but it was only after Kosta pressed a considerable sum of money into the bishop's palm that everything fell into place and the wedding was able to proceed.

Extremely hot, dry weather meant that the water supply in Thessaloniki was strictly rationed and it was turned off every day between the hours of 8 am and 8 pm. On the wedding day, we had to fill up buckets of water early in the morning and sit them in the sun on the balcony all day so that I could bathe in a bucket before going to my wedding.

The entire village made the trip to Thessaloniki for the wedding. The ceremony was in ancient Greek and they could have been taking me to my execution for all that I knew. There was no seating in the church and friends and relatives stood around us, as the priest led us three times around the altar, symbolising the dance which the prophet Isaiah is recorded to have danced, when told that God would take on human form. Kosta and I were crowned as king and queen of our home and family, rings were exchanged and we were pronounced husband and wife. Incidentally, they forgot to tell me that instead of saying, 'You may now kiss the bride,' in the Greek marriage service the new husband stands on his wife's toes – so she knows who's the boss!

After the ceremony, we returned to the Electra Palace hotel in Salonika to change clothes for the reception. A brass band was playing at the front of the hotel, and as we stepped out of the wedding car, into the music, it seemed that they played only for us.

Music and dance are a vitally important part of all Greek celebrations. At village weddings, the groom's friends, together with a band of local musicians, will dance him to the church, taking the longest, slowest route through the village streets, in a symbolic attempt at preventing him from marrying and leaving their company.

Greeks love to dance. It is an expression of love, passion and happiness. At every celebration the women join arms and form circles, dancing delicate steps. Or a lone young man will dance his story of lost love, while his friends squat around him in a circle, clapping out the rhythm to the violin or a mournful clarinet.

There can be no celebration without a feast, although our wedding feast consisted of relatively simple fare – mezzethes with ouzo, roast kid and potatoes, horiatiki salad with retsina, and plates of peponi, a deliciously sweet, creamy green melon for dessert.

It was a wonderful night. Kosta and I danced for hours and after we left the restaurant we sat on the balcony outside our room at the Electra Palace looking out over the city lights and watching the ships in the bay until the early hours of the morning.

Mezze

A Greek meal starts with mezze (or mezzethes), a selection of appetisers that are traditionally served on individual small plates with bread and a glass of ouzo or tsiporo, the local anise-flavoured spirit.

Along the water's edge on the islands, a line strung with octopus drying in the sun is a common sight, together with those picture postcards shops with rattan seated chairs and little square blue and green painted wooden tables, where a single dish is on offer, maybe grilled (broiled) octopus or chargrilled sardines, salad and bread. Down the back there is a sink to wash hands and a few barrels of ouzo and retsina, the ouzo served in a peninteraki (50 ml/1¾ fl oz bottles of ouzo) and the retsina brought to the table in an aluminium pitcher.

In larger towns one finds mezzethopoleion – restaurants dedicated to the preparation and service of mezzethes where one can make a whole meal of small dishes, picking and grazing for hours.

Mezzethes may be as simple as a few batons of cucumber, some anchovies and a slice of bread. But more often, for a family occasion, the table will be laden with plates of grilled (broiled) sardines or anchovies, fried capsicums (peppers), eggplant (aubergine) and zucchini (courgette), tzatziki, fried cheese balls, stuffed olives, dolmades, taramosalata, melitzanosalata, salads of sliced tomato, cucumber and feta and of course, hearty slices of horiatiko psomi (village bread).

Many mezze dishes have a salty component to stimulate the appetite and encourage the continued consumption of drinks: olives, anchovies and taramosalata are common.

In our village in Greece most families have their own vineyard, or ampeli. It is usually about 1000 square metres (a quarter-acre) of manicured vines, which are tended with the utmost care to produce grapes for making tsiporo. In October the village still goes into production, everyone's grapes are pressed and distilled, the nights get cooler and much tsiporo is consumed.

The consumption of mezzethes with tsiporo is a lengthy and relaxed experience which is not to be undertaken in a rush. In every village square, especially on Saturdays and Sundays, groups of friends, mainly men, pass the midday hours in conversation around tables laden with plates of mezzethes and peninterakis before wandering off home for a siesta in the mid-afternoon. This is an extremely important part of the community social life.

And in the evening, while the women sit together on their verandas after the day's chores are done, crocheting, discussing food and families and offering a gliko (a spoonful of preserved fruit), the men will gather at the local café for a game of backgammon, a coffee or a peninteraki of ouzo and a few mezze dishes.

ABOVE *From left, Eggplant Salad; Tzatziki; Taramosalata.*

Tzatziki

Greek people eat a lot of yoghurt. It is a standard part of the daily diet, eaten on its own as a meal for breakfast or supper, as an accompaniment to vegetable dishes such as Koukia (page 93) or Sarmathakia (page 55), and as a mezze, usually in the form of tzatziki.

Tzatziki is most often made using finely chopped or grated cucumber and dill, and do feel free to substitute these in the recipe that follows. My personal preference, though, is to use thinly sliced cucumber for more substance, and for the fresh tang of mint that complements the slight acidity of the yoghurt.

....

650 g (1 lb 7 oz) yoghurt
1 cucumber
1 clove garlic, finely chopped
½ cup mint leaves, finely chopped
125 ml (4 fl oz) extra virgin olive oil
½ teaspoon salt
½ teaspoon freshly ground black pepper

Tip the yoghurt into a colander lined with a clean piece of muslin (cheesecloth). Sit the colander in a bowl and leave in a cool place to drain for a few hours. Discard the liquid and tip the yoghurt into a clean mixing bowl.

Peel the cucumber and cut it in half lengthwise. Use a teaspoon to remove the seeds, leaving a hollow centre. With a sharp knife, cut fine slices on the diagonal, like half-moons. Place these in a colander for a few minutes to drain away excess liquid.

Add the cucumber, garlic, mint, olive oil and seasonings to the yoghurt. Fold in gently but thoroughly, then taste and adjust the seasonings to your liking.

Makes about 700 g (1 lb 9 oz)

Eggplant salad
Melitzanosalata

This is a popular dish in many Middle Eastern countries where it is known by a variety of names. Melitzanosalata translates from Greek simply as 'eggplant (aubergine) salad'. It is typically served as an appetiser and can be eaten on a slice of bread as a snack, but melitzanosalata also marries perfectly with chargrilled lamb.

To ensure a lovely pale colour, make sure you buy very fresh shiny eggplants and peel them as soon as they've been cooked – don't let them sit in their skins or they will discolour. The salad will keep in the fridge for three or four days.

....

3 large firm eggplants (aubergines)
3 cloves garlic, finely chopped
½ cup flat-leaf (Italian) parsley
125 ml (4 fl oz) extra virgin olive oil
salt
freshly ground black pepper
125 g (4½ oz) feta cheese, crumbled

Prick the eggplants all over with a sharp knife and cook over charcoals or on a barbecue until the skin has charred and the flesh is soft. Peel the skin away immediately, while holding the eggplants under cold running water. Place the peeled eggplants in a colander to drain for at least 1 hour.

Chop the eggplant flesh roughly and place in a mixing bowl with the garlic, parsley, olive oil, salt and pepper. Whisk until the mixture is well combined and glossy. Fold in the crumbled feta.

Makes about 500 g (1 lb 2 oz)

Taramosalata

Nearly everyone knows this salty pink Greek dip. It's traditionally made from grey mullet roe, but these days most commercial versions are made from other fish roe, such as cod or ling. Keep tasting as you make it to get a good balance between the flavours. You may need to add more lemon juice.

Taramosalata is delicious served with batons of cucumber, some warm golden Piadina bread (page 184) and a glass of ouzo.

....

¼ onion
3 cloves garlic
2 thick slices stale white bread, crusts removed
2 egg yolks
1 heaped tablespoon tarama (available from
    Greek delicatessens and some supermarkets)
600 ml (20 fl oz) vegetable oil
200 ml (7 fl oz) lemon juice
½ teaspoon sumac

In a food processor, whiz the onion, garlic and bread until very finely chopped. Add the egg yolks and incorporate briefly, then the tarama. With the motor on, slowly pour in the vegetable oil, until the mixture is thick and turns pink and creamy. Add lemon juice to taste and to adjust the consistency to a glossy, fairly thick dip. Serve topped with a sprinkling of sumac.

Makes about 750 g (1 lb 11 oz)

Braised eggplant with cumin and tomato

Eggplants (aubergines) are one of the most versatile summer vegetables. They can be stuffed, chargrilled, fried, cooked with other vegetables in Tourlou (page 95) and made into many types of dips. This dish is perfect served hot with grilled (broiled) lamb chops or served cold as a mezze, or as a salad to accompany any number of fish or meat dishes. Make it as spicy as you like by adding more or less chilli.

....

2 eggplants (aubergines)
salt
125 ml (4 fl oz) extra virgin olive oil
3 cloves garlic, chopped
1 bullet chilli
1 teaspoon ground cumin
3 ripe tomatoes, halved and coarsely grated,
    skins discarded
1 teaspoon sugar
125 ml (4 fl oz) lemon juice
freshly ground black pepper

Cut the eggplant into 3 cm (1¼ in) cubes, sprinkle with salt and sit in a colander. Leave for an hour then rinse thoroughly and pat dry.

Heat the oil in a heavy-based saucepan and fry the eggplant in batches until evenly coloured on all sides. Add the garlic, chilli and cumin and stir well. Stir in the tomato pulp, then add the sugar and lemon juice and season to taste. Cook over a low heat for about 2 hours, stirring frequently to prevent the mixture from sticking to the bottom of the pan. The eggplant pieces should be cooked until completely breaking up and mushy.

Makes about 500 g (1 lb 2 oz)

Salt cod croquettes

This recipe comes from Moro, a restaurant in London, which was set up by our friend Michael Benyan. The croquettes are probably Spanish in origin, but fit well into all Mediterranean cuisines, because of the similarities in eating styles and available ingredients. We like to serve them as a mezze with a dipping sauce or mayonnaise such as aïoli.

450 g (1 lb) salt cod
600 ml (20½ fl oz) milk
2 onions, sliced
2 cloves garlic
6 whole black peppercorns
4 potatoes, quartered

2 eggs
½ cup chopped flat-leaf (Italian) parsley leaves
plain (all purpose) flour
vegetable oil for frying
Aïoli (page 161) to serve

Soak the salt cod in cold water for at least 24 hours, changing the water three times.

Pour the milk into a heavy-based saucepan and add the onions, garlic and peppercorns. Bring to the boil then add the potatoes. Boil until the potatoes are soft, then lift them out with a slotted spoon and set aside.

Place the salt cod in the hot milk then return it to the boil and cook for 15 minutes. When the fish is cooked, remove the pan from the heat and allow to cool.

Remove and discard the bones and skin from the fish and transfer it to a mixing bowl. Add the cooked potatoes, eggs and parsley and beat with a fork to make a smooth mixture. Use two spoons to form the mixture into croquettes. Roll them in flour so they are evenly coated.

Heat the oil in a medium saucepan and deep-fry the croquettes until golden brown all over. Drain on kitchen paper and serve hot with aïoli.

Serves 8

Baked beans Fassolia fourno

In Greece these beans are mostly served as an appetiser or mezze, but I think they also make a delicious breakfast or lunch, with a slice of toasted sourdough and a piece of feta. You need a lot of oil to create a lovely rich sauce and the dish should not be watery.

....

500 g (1 lb 2 oz) dried cannellini or butterbeans (lima beans)
1 onion, diced
1 carrot, diced
1 stalk celery, diced
1 tablespoon tomato paste (concentrated purée)

3 cloves garlic, finely chopped
2 teaspoons chopped chilli
½ cup flat-leaf (Italian) parsley, finely chopped
2 teaspoons salt
1 teaspoon freshly ground black pepper
375 ml (12 ½ fl oz) extra virgin olive oil

Wash the beans to remove any dust or little stones. Cover generously with cold water and soak overnight. The next day, drain the beans and tip them into a large saucepan. Cover generously with fresh cold water and bring to the boil. Add the onion, carrot and celery and simmer for 30–45 minutes, or until the beans can be squashed between your thumb and forefinger.

Preheat the oven to 180°C (350°F).

Strain the beans, reserving 500 ml (17 fl oz) of the liquid. Pour the beans into a baking tray. Dissolve the tomato paste in the reserved cooking liquid then stir it evenly through the beans. Add the garlic, chilli, parsley, salt and pepper and stir to combine. Pour the olive oil over the top and bake for 1 hour, by which time all the liquid should be absorbed, and there should be a layer of golden oil on top.

Serves 8

Dolmades

These are delicious made in the spring when the first young leaves appear on the grapevines. Dolmades are best made from the leaves of wine grapes rather than table grapes, as the latter have more pronounced jagged edges and do not wrap up so well into neat little parcels.

In Greek families, dolmades are kept in the fridge for snacks and when friends come to visit they are served as a mezze or an appetiser.

500 g (1 lb 2 oz) fresh vine leaves, or a jar of vine leaves preserved in brine
450 g (1 lb) medium-grain rice, rinsed until the water runs clear
10 spring onions (scallions), finely chopped
½ cup dill, finely chopped
½ cup mint leaves, finely chopped

juice of 1 lemon
315 ml (10 ½ fl oz) extra virgin olive oil
2 teaspoons salt
1 teaspoon freshly ground black pepper
1 litre (34 fl oz) water
plain yoghurt to serve

If using fresh vine leaves, blanch them, a few at a time, in a large saucepan of boiling water. Refresh in cold water then lay them flat on a tea (dish) towel to dry. Trim off the stalks with sharp scissors. If using preserved leaves, rinse them well to remove the brine. Dry and trim off the stalks, as for the fresh leaves.

In a large mixing bowl, combine the rice, spring onions, herbs, lemon juice and 190 ml (6 ½ fl oz) of the olive oil. Season with salt and pepper and mix everything together well.

Lay a vine leaf out on the back of a dinner plate, with the vein side up. Place a spoonful of the rice mixture across the base of the leaf. Roll it over once, fold the sides in and then continue to roll into a neat sausage shape. The dolmades should be about the size of a finger – don't roll them too tightly or they will burst during the cooking. Repeat until all the rice mixture is used up. You should have a few vine leaves left over.

Lay a few of the remaining vine leaves flat over the base of a large saucepan. Pack the dolmades tightly into the pan then add more layers until all are used. Pour on the water and the remaining 125 ml (4 fl oz) of olive oil. Lie a few more vine leaves over the dolmades then sit a plate on top and cover the pan with a lid. Cook over a medium heat for 1 hour then remove from the heat and leave to cool in the pan. Drain and serve the dolmades at room temperature with yoghurt.

Makes 30–40

Dolmades with minced pork Sarmathakia

This version of dolmades is made with meat filling and is often eaten as a main meal rather than a mezze or snack. They are usually served with avgolemono, which is a Greek version of hollandaise sauce.

500 g (1 lb 2 oz) fresh vine leaves, or a jar of vine leaves preserved in brine
500 g (1 lb 2 oz) minced (ground) pork
2 small–medium onions, diced
½ cup dill, finely chopped
½ cup mint leaves, finely chopped
juice of 1 lemon

250 g (9 oz) medium-grain rice, rinsed until the water runs clear
2 teaspoons salt
1 teaspoon freshly ground black pepper
315 ml (10 ½ fl oz) extra virgin olive oil
750 ml (25 fl oz) water
Avgolemono (page 160) to serve

If using fresh vine leaves, blanch them, a few at a time, in a large saucepan of boiling water. Refresh in cold water then lay them flat on a tea (dish) towel to dry. Trim off the stalks with sharp scissors. If using preserved leaves, rinse them well to remove the brine. Dry and trim off the stalks, as for the fresh leaves.

In a large mixing bowl, combine the minced pork, onion, herbs, lemon juice, rice and seasonings with 190 ml (6 ½ fl oz) of the olive oil. Mix with your hands until well combined.

Prepare the dolmades as described opposite.

Lay a few vine leaves flat over the base of a large saucepan. Pack the dolmades tightly into the pan, then add more layers until all are used. Pour on the water and the remaining 125 ml (4 fl oz) of olive oil. Lay a few more vine leaves over the dolmades then sit a plate on top and cover the pan with a lid. Cook over a medium heat for 1 hour then remove from the heat and leave to cool in the pan. Serve the dolmades warm or at room temperature with avgolemono.

Makes 30–40

Long yellow peppers stuffed with feta

This tasty lunch dish is very easy to prepare. The sauce that forms in the pan from the cooking juices and feta is delicious mopped up with some bread. Choose the large mild Hungarian wax peppers that are about 20 cm (8 in) long.

12 long yellow or red wax peppers
1 kg (2 lb 3 oz) feta cheese
4 ripe tomatoes, sliced

freshly ground black pepper
190 ml (6 ½ fl oz) extra virgin olive oil

Preheat the oven to 180°C (350°F) and lightly oil a baking tray.

Slice the stem ends off the peppers and use the point of a sharp knife to scrape out the seeds inside, keeping the peppers whole.

Cut the feta into pieces about 2 cm x 2 cm x 8 cm (¾ in x ¾ in x 3 ¼ in). Don't worry too much if it crumbles. Push a piece of feta inside each pepper, inserting it as far as you can.

Lay the peppers flat on the baking tray, so they fit snugly together. Top with slices of tomato and sprinkle with pepper. Drizzle with oil and bake for 50 minutes, or until the peppers are lightly coloured.

Serves 4

Tomato with feta and hot peppers Bouyourdi

This dish combines some of my favourite textures and flavours: sweet tomatoes, melting salty feta, and crunchy hot peppers. Look for the type of long yellow peppers that have a bit of heat, but if you can't find them, use a roasted red capsicum (pepper) together with a roasted green chilli or bullet chilli. You don't want to overpower the dish with chilli, but need just enough heat to excite the taste buds. Serve as a part of a mezze selection.

....

2 tablespoons extra virgin olive oil
2 ripe tomatoes, cored and cut into thick slices

2 long yellow wax peppers, halved lengthwise, stems and seeds removed
250 g (9 oz) feta cheese, cut into 4 pieces

Heat the oil in a heavy-based frying pan or saganaki pan. Add the tomatoes and peppers and fry for 5 minutes until they are starting to colour and soften. Add the pieces of feta, tucking them in between the tomato and peppers. Cook on a low heat for 5 minutes until the feta is soft and melted. Serve immediately straight from the saganaki pan.

Serves 4

....

Kephalograviera baked in vine leaves with cherry tomatoes

Kephalograviera is a hard, salty sheep's milk cheese available from Greek delicatessens. Grilled (broiled) kephalograviera is served in Greek restaurants around the world, and in Australia is better known as saganaki, after the pan in which it is usually cooked and served. Kephalograviera is generally eaten hot. It can be grated onto pasta and rice dishes, or grilled and served on bruschetta. In this dish, the cheese melts inside a wrapping of vine leaves, which have their own distinctive flavour. The sweet juiciness of the roasted cherry tomatoes counteracts the saltiness of the cheese.

....

8 vine leaves preserved in brine
500 g (1 lb 2 oz) cherry tomatoes on the stem
190 ml (6 ½ fl oz) extra virgin olive oil
salt

freshly ground black pepper
400 g (14 oz) kephalograviera, cut into 4 slices, each about 10 cm x 2 cm (4 in x ¾ in)

Preheat the oven to 200°C (400°F).

Rinse the vine leaves well to remove the brine, then drain. Dry and trim off the stalks.

Cut the cherry tomatoes into small bunches of three or four tomatoes. Place in a small baking tray, drizzle with 2 tablespoons of the oil and season with salt and pepper. Bake for 12 minutes.

Lay two large vine leaves out on a work surface so they overlap. Brush with a little oil and place a slice of cheese on top. Wrap the leaves tightly around the cheese to form a neat parcel. Repeat with more vine leaves and the remaining slices of cheese to make a total of 4 parcels.

Brush each parcel with a little more oil and bake for 8–10 minutes until the vine leaves colour and the cheese is soft. Alternatively, cook under a very hot grill (broiler) or on a griddle plate. Serve with the roasted cherry tomatoes and eat straight away while hot as the kephalograviera becomes stiff when it gets cold.

Serves 4

Chargrilled garlic mussels

Whenever possible I prefer to use local mussels, instead of the widely available green-lipped mussels that are imported from New Zealand. Locally caught mussels will always be fresher and plumper, which is especially important in this dish. Remember that mussels are seasonal: they spawn late in the spring then take a few months to build up condition again. They are at their best from autumn and through winter to early spring.

Use any combination of fresh herbs for this dish, especially if you grow them in your garden. Chervil is a particularly good substitute for parsley, and is very easy to grow. Dill is also a good match with mussels. It has a strong flavour that complements the saltiness of the mussels very well. If you like a bit of heat, add a teaspoon of finely chopped chilli to the garlic and herbs.

....

1 kg (2 lb 3 oz) black mussels, scrubbed clean and
   beards removed
125 ml (4 fl oz) extra virgin olive oil
60 g (2 oz) butter

3 cloves garlic, finely chopped
1 tablespoon chopped parsley
1 tablespoon chopped dill

Preheat a barbecue or griddle to high.

Spread the mussels out over the heat. As soon as they begin to open, remove them from the heat and place them in a bowl. Take care not to overcook them or they will dry out. Discard any mussels that don't open after 4–5 minutes on the heat. When they are cool enough to handle, break off the top shell, leaving the mussel meat attached to the bottom shell.

Heat the oil and butter in a frying pan until beginning to froth. Add the garlic and herbs and sauté until the garlic begins to colour.

Arrange the mussels in their shells on a serving plate and pour the garlicky butter over the top.

Serves 4

Prawn saganaki with tomato, feta and basil

In Australia the word 'saganaki' has become synonymous with a type of cheese, but it is actually the word for a small, shallow, two-handled pan in which the cheese is often cooked. A saganaki is used for many dishes that are cooked in the oven or on the stovetop and then served directly at the table. You don't have to use a saganaki pan to cook this dish, of course, an ovenproof frying pan will do just as well.

I like to use medium–large king prawns (jumbo shrimp) that are caught in Port Lincoln in South Australia and snap-frozen straight away on the boats. They are very meaty and have a great flavour.

....

16 king prawns (jumbo shrimp) (4 per person)
salt
80 ml (3 fl oz) extra virgin olive oil
3 cloves garlic, finely chopped
200 ml (7 fl oz) white wine

6 ripe tomatoes, peeled and diced
1 handful basil leaves, chopped
freshly ground black pepper
200 g (7 oz) feta cheese, cut into 12 cm x 3 cm
    (4 ¾ in x 1 ¼ in) cubes

Heat the oven to 200°C (400°F).

Shell the prawns, leaving the heads and tails intact. With a sharp knife, split each prawn along the back and carefully pull out the intestinal tube. Sprinkle the prawns lightly with salt.

Heat the oil in a large frying pan. Add the prawns in batches and sauté on a medium-high heat for 2 minutes on each side, until pink and starting to turn crisp and golden brown. Add the garlic to the pan and sauté for 1 minute. Add the wine and cook for 1 minute until slightly reduced. Remove the prawns from the pan, dividing them evenly among 4 saganaki pans or an ovenproof dish.

Add the diced tomatoes and basil to the frying pan and season with pepper. Cook for a couple of minutes, until the tomatoes are warmed through, then spoon over the prawns. Add 3 pieces of feta to each saganaki, or tuck them in among the prawns if using a large pan. Transfer to the oven for 5 minutes, until the cheese begins to soften. Take to the table to serve.

Serves 4

Pickled octopus

A common sight in many seaside villages in Greece is a row of octopus strung up to dry along the edge of the water, like washing on a washing line. In southern parts of Australia we are very fortunate to have a ready supply of large octopus as a by-product of the crayfish industry. At A la Grecque we never use imported frozen baby octopus from Asia because the local product is far superior.

A freshly caught octopus needs to be tenderised before it is cooked. For instant tenderising — if you have the energy — it can be bashed on the rocks at the water's edge. But octopus is more commonly tenderised by freezing it for a couple of days. The water in the cells expands as it freezes, breaking down the cell walls and softening the flesh.

When handling a large octopus, I try to pull off as much of the blackish outer membrane as possible before cooking, as it is very difficult to remove after cooking without pulling the suckers off the tentacles. I like the suckers to remain intact on the tentacles, for presentation more than anything else. I feel it adds authenticity and interest to the dish.

This dish is quite rich and filling, so serve in small portions. It goes particularly well with a Bread and Tomato Salad (page 80).

1 x 2 kg (4 lb 6 oz) whole ocean octopus
1 stalk celery, leaves attached, roughly chopped
1 onion, roughly chopped
6 cloves garlic
a handful of black peppercorns
500 ml (17 fl oz) white wine vinegar
6 stalks parsley
1 bay leaf

Dressing
125 ml (4 fl oz) extra virgin olive oil
2 tablespoons white wine vinegar
salt
freshly ground black pepper
⅓ cup finely chopped parsley
⅓ cup finely chopped dill

Wash the octopus and remove the beak. Turn the head inside out and wash away the contents. Pull away the black outer skin from the tentacles and cut them off the head. Place all the bits and pieces in a large saucepan with the vegetables, garlic, peppercorns, vinegar and herbs. It may not look as if there is much liquid, but the octopus will release a lot of liquid as it cooks. Cover the saucepan and bring to the boil. Lower the heat and simmer gently for 40 minutes, stirring occasionally to prevent the ingredients from sticking to the bottom of the pan.

Test the octopus with a sharp knife. It should be quite tender. Lift it out of the pan and discard the remaining ingredients and cooking liquid. Leave the octopus to cool then cut into 3 cm (1¼ in) pieces.

Whisk the dressing ingredients together and pour over the cold octopus. Serve as a starter with Bread and Tomato Salad.

Serves 8

Stuffed kalamari with rice and herbs

Clean the kalamari as described on page 113, or ask your fishmonger to do this for you. You don't need the tentacles for this recipe, so keep them for another meal.

For this recipe it is important to measure the rice out by volume (allow ½ tablespoon of rice for each kalamari). You need exactly double that volume of water for cooking (so for 1 cup of rice you will need 500 ml (17 fl oz) water) plus an extra 190 ml (6 ½ fl oz) to create the sauce.

....

1 cup medium grain rice
250 ml (8 ½ fl oz) extra virgin olive oil
8 spring onions (scallions), finely chopped
2 cloves garlic, finely chopped
½ cup chopped dill
½ cup chopped flat-leaf (Italian) parsley leaves

1 teaspoon salt
½ teaspoon ground black pepper
8 x 15 cm (6 in) kalamari (body sac only)
2 teaspoons tomato paste (concentrated purée)
690 ml (23 ½ fl oz) water

Rinse the rice under cold running water until the water runs clear. Drain.

Heat 2 tablespoons of the oil in a heavy-based saucepan. Add the spring onions and sauté gently for about 8 minutes, until soft and translucent. Add the garlic and herbs, followed by the rice. Season with salt and pepper and stir together well. Fry for 1 minute, stirring, then remove the pan from the heat and leave to cool for a few minutes.

Place a tablespoonful of the rice mixture into each kalamari tube and secure at the open end with a strong toothpick or bamboo skewer.

Layer the stuffed kalamari tubes into a heavy-based pot or casserole dish. Dissolve the tomato paste in a little of the measured water and pour over the kalamari. Add the rest of the water and the remaining olive oil. Cover the pan with a tight-fitting lid and bring to the boil. Lower the heat and simmer gently for 40 minutes, by which time the rice and kalamari will both be cooked. Serve in shallow bowls, spooning some of the cooking liquid from the bottom of the pot over the kalamari.

Serves 4

Village life

After a busy season at A la Grecque, Kosta
and I look forward with eager anticipation
to closing up the restaurant and catching
the plane to Greece for a well-earned
holiday. We have another life there and we
step back into it with ease.

But our house has been shut up over the northern winter months and we arrive to find mould in the sinks and dust and cobwebs in every corner. The garden is bare, weeds have choked the flower beds and piles of leaves have accumulated on the veranda. As soon as we arrive, we set to work, so that we can at least have a hot bath and put clean sheets on the bed. Next comes a good night's sleep, and the following day our Greek life begins again in earnest.

It is springtime in the village when we arrive and the nights are cold. But the mornings sparkle and we rise early and walk to the next village. Blood-red poppies line the roadside, fields of green wheat sway in the breeze, and we greet old friends who liken our reappearance to the swallows, heralding the imminent return of summer.

We have to work quickly to get the garden in order, if we are to enjoy the full harvest before we return to Australia in August. Local markets are full of seedlings for sale and we are unable to resist them. We usually buy far more than we need, but it is our joy to fill every space in the garden. The villagers tend their gardens every day, sharing early produce with us and offering us seedlings of every sort. In return, I bring a box of unusual heirloom seed varieties from Australia and share these around. They are welcomed by many, but treated with scepticism by the die-hards who prefer the tried and true Greek varieties.

Once the garden is planted, we wait for signs of life, checking every day for tiny sprouts of lettuce seedlings, or to see the earth cracking to reveal a bean shoot, curled ready to spring up and face the sun. The cherry trees are laden with fruit and the swallows dart in and out all day long.

Life for the village women is all about food: growing it, preparing it, eating it and sharing it. They ask each other, 'What are you cooking today?', 'How did your jam work out?', 'Today I'm making bread … yoghurt … cheese'.

Every day small vans pass through the village streets selling goods of every kind. Music blares out from loud speakers and sets of old-fashioned scales swing from the back.

....

The fishmonger comes early in the morning. Another van sells rice of every possible colour and shape while others sell flour and sugar, watermelons, peaches, furniture, rugs or shoes. Many of the older village people have no car and rely on these roaming produce trucks for their everyday goods.

Our days in the village also revolve around planning and preparing the evening meal. As well as the produce trucks, there are markets held in one or other of the surrounding local villages on every day of the week. We look for the freshest fish and plan our dinner around that, deciding which salads, vegetables and fruit to buy. Olives, cheeses and wine are all on our shopping list.

Our village neighours consume their main meal in the middle of the day, followed by a siesta. In the evenings they only eat a bowl of yoghurt or trakhana, so we are considered a curiosity as we light the barbecue, lay the table under the grapevine-covered pergola and open a bottle of wine. On the streets people are out and about, strolling in the evening air, visiting friends, gossiping and relaxing after the day's work is over. Friends and neighbours drop by to see us, happily sharing a glass of wine and a bite from our table – there's always plenty.

Within a few weeks our garden is overflowing with food. The warm climate and fertile limestone soil in the village are a magical combination and soon we are eating lettuces, capsicums (peppers), tomatoes and beans. I make vegetable casseroles such as tourlou, fassolakia and koukia, using whatever I pick in the morning, lots of lovely olive oil, herbs and of course a big slice of feta.

Growing produce in our vegetable garden in Lorne is another story. It has taken me years of digging truck-loads of manure, straw and compost into the naturally poor soil to build up tillable, friable garden beds. And then, just when I've got an amazing crop of corn or tomatoes and am busy planning the next meal, I find the lot senselessly destroyed by flocks of greedy parrots and destructive cockatoos. It's heartbreaking – and it should be enough to make one give up altogether. But hope springs eternal, and each new season I plant more crops with a prayer, 'Maybe this time!'

Despite the obstacles, I do manage to grow a number of vegetables in abundance: beans, zucchini (courgettes), cabbage, cucumbers, lettuce and root vegetables thrive. The excess, which we can't consume at home, is taken to the restaurant and incorporated into the menu, along with herbs and fresh free-range eggs.

Salads and vegetables

The benefits of a diet based primarily on vegetables, olive oil and fish are well documented and the Mediterranean diet is widely recognised for its health-giving properties.

In our Greek village all the women and many of the men are devout church-goers. The Orthodox Church prescribes fasting days before many of the holy festivals and saint name days, as well as prohibiting the eating of meat on Wednesdays and Fridays. My mother-in-law, Yiayia, followed these dictates to the letter and would organise the family's meals to be vegan on all of the prescribed fasting days. As our children got older they started objecting to this, so she would prepare a normal meal for the family, and then make a point of sitting down to dinner with one boiled potato on her own plate.

In Greece meat is expensive and is eaten only once or twice a week. Arable land is too precious to be left uncultivated for grazing animals and instead they are grazed by a shepherd in a communal flock, roaming the edges of the roads and along the river in the evenings. Each paddock is farmed intensively and crops are rotated to alternately fertilise and rest the soil. Rocket (arugula) and broccoli are now being grown commercially in the village as farmers have been forced to diversify, with the European Union withdrawing its subsidies for tobacco and cotton, previously the main crops grown in the area.

Every family in the village has a vegetable garden and aims to be as self-sufficient as possible.

Children arrive from the city at the weekends and leave with the car full of fresh fruit and vegetables from the family garden as well as containers of cooked casseroles and pita breads, lovingly prepared during the week and frozen for transport.

Spinach is grown in abundance and is used to make spanakoriso (spinach and rice) and spanakotiropita (spinach pie), or is added to soups. Dill, parsley, spring onions (scallions) and green garlic are essential ingredients in most spring vegetable dishes and salads. Greens of all kinds (including dandelions, amaranth, endive/chicory and beetroot/beet leaves), known as horta, are grown in gardens or gathered from the paddocks. They are steamed and served with a generous amount of olive oil and lemon juice, as a salad.

Spring and summer bring an abundance of vegetables to the Greek table in the form of casseroles eaten with bread and feta cheese. These are generically called lathera, from the Greek word 'lathi' meaning olive oil, as the vegetables are stewed in their own juices, with olive oil and herbs and sometimes with tomatoes. These dishes can be a mixture of many vegetables such as tourlou, or made with one particular vegetable such as broad (fava) beans (koukia), green beans (fassolakia) or okra (bamyies). To many Australians, these dishes seem to be overcooked as we are used to eating vegetables steamed, or slightly crunchy. But they are delicious, as the flavours cook together and you mop up the juices with a crust of bread.

Chargrilled eggplant, red capsicum, tomato, onion, parsley Konstantinopoli salata

This salad originated in Kiz Dervent, the village in Turkey where my parents-in-law were born. Back in the early days of the 20th century, when they were small children, the horseback journey to the capital, Konstantinopoli, was a rare excursion for most of the village people. In those days, few villagers had the opportunity or the means to venture outside of the village, especially the women, who, still to this day, hardly ever leave the house.

Clearly some brave soul did make the trip though, and on his return to the village enthused over the salad which he had eaten in the city. From then on, the village women referred to the dish as Constantinople Salad. It is a colourful combination of sweet, ripe summer vegetables, which have a wonderful smoky aroma as a result of cooking over charcoals. If you don't have a charcoal grill, then a barbecue will work well.

....

2 firm, shiny eggplants (aubergines)
2 red capsicums (peppers)
3 ripe tomatoes
1 red (Spanish) onion, sliced into rings
1 cup flat-leaf (Italian) parsley leaves

125 ml (4 fl oz) extra virgin olive oil
2 tablespoons red wine vinegar
salt
freshly ground black pepper

Prick the eggplants all over with a sharp knife. Cook both the eggplants and capsicums over charcoals or on a barbecue until the skins have charred and the flesh is soft.

Remove the eggplants from the heat and immediately peel away the skins while holding them under gently running cold water. Place the peeled eggplants in a colander to drain for at least 1 hour.

Transfer the capsicums to a bowl and cover with plastic wrap. When cool enough to handle, peel them and remove the seeds.

Bring a large saucepan of water to the boil. Cut a small cross in the base of each tomato and drop them carefully into the boiling water. Remove after 30 seconds and refresh immediately in iced water. This will make it easier to slip off the skins. Slice the tomatoes into wedges and place them in a serving bowl.

When ready to make the salad, cut the eggplant flesh into 3 cm (1 ¼ in) pieces and the capsicums into 3 cm (1 ¼ in) squares. Add to the serving bowl with the tomato wedges, onion and parsley.

Whisk the oil and vinegar together and season with salt and pepper. Pour over the salad and toss everything together gently.

Serves 4

....

Bread and tomato salad

The beauty of this salad is that the crunchy bread soaks up all the flavoursome juices from the tomatoes, capsicums (peppers) and extra virgin olive oil. We often serve this salad with Pickled Octopus (page 64). The two dishes combine brilliantly with their sweet, tangy and salty flavours, and crunchy, chewy and smooth textures.

   It is rather time-consuming to prepare, but most of the preparation, such as roasting and peeling the capsicums, blanching the tomatoes and toasting the bread, can be done the day before. All you need to do then is to assemble the ingredients and serve.

2 red capsicums (peppers)
3 slices sourdough bread, cut into 2 cm cubes
125 ml (4 fl oz) extra virgin olive oil
3 ripe tomatoes
1 red (Spanish) onion, sliced

3 anchovies, roughly chopped
⅓ cup capers, well rinsed
a handful of basil leaves, roughly torn
freshly ground black pepper

Preheat the oven to 180°C (350°F).

Roast the capsicums for 40 minutes, or until the skin has browned and the flesh is very soft. Transfer to a bowl and cover with plastic wrap. When cool enough to handle, peel the capsicums and remove the seeds. Don't be tempted to rinse them in water or you will wash away all the flavoursome juices. Cut into 3 cm (1¼ in) squares.

Drizzle the bread with about half the olive oil and bake for 8–10 minutes, or until golden brown and crunchy.

Bring a large saucepan of water to the boil. Cut a small cross in the base of each tomato and drop them carefully into the boiling water. Remove after 30 seconds and refresh immediately in iced water. Slip off the skins and cut the tomatoes into 3 cm (1¼ in) dice.

Combine the capsicums, bread, tomatoes, onion, anchovies, capers and basil in a large mixing bowl. Drizzle on the remaining olive oil and season with pepper. There is no need to add salt as both the anchovies and capers are salty. Toss gently and serve straight away so the bread is still crunchy.

Serves 6

Cucumber, radish, red onion and caperi salad

At A la Grecque we serve this salad with finely sliced gravadlax. It combines beautifully with the strong flavour of the salmon, and the crisp texture and vibrant colours are also very pleasing. Serve this salad as soon as you have made it, so that the ingredients are crisp. It does not benefit from sitting around.

Caperi are baby capers, which are generally sold packed in salt. They must be thoroughly rinsed in cold water and drained before using.

....

1 telegraph (long) cucumber
6 red radishes, finely sliced into rings
½ red (Spanish) onion, finely sliced into rings
2 tablespoons caperi, rinsed and drained

2 tablespoons white wine vinegar
2 tablespoons extra virgin olive oil
½ teaspoon salt
½ teaspoon sugar

Use a vegetable peeler to slice the cucumber lengthways into ribbons. Leave the skin on but discard the seeds when you reach the centre.

Combine the cucumber ribbons with the radishes, onion and caperi in a serving bowl. Whisk together the vinegar, oil, salt and sugar. Spoon over the salad and serve immediately.

Serves 6

Beetroot salad with yoghurt and mint

This brightly coloured and refreshing salad goes perfectly with grilled fish – especially oily fish, such as mackerel or sardines. It can also be used as a dip to serve with crudités as a starter.

....

1 medium beetroot (beet), peeled and grated
400 g (14 oz) Labne (page 89)
1 clove garlic, finely chopped
½ cup mint leaves, finely chopped

125 ml (4 fl oz) extra virgin olive oil
salt
freshly ground black pepper

Discard any liquid that seeps from the grated beetroot. Place it in a mixing bowl with the labne, garlic and mint leaves. Add the olive oil and stir well so that everything is evenly combined. Season to taste with salt and pepper.

Serves 8–10

....

Fried zucchini with aïoli

Zucchini (courgettes) are one of the easiest vegetables to grow. If you pick them daily, or as soon as they reach about 15 cm (6 in) long, and don't allow any to reach mammoth proportions, your plants will continue to bear fruit all through the summer and autumn. More troublesome is what to do with all the zucchini you harvest. I find this recipe is a very easy and tasty way to use some of those zucchini that you have accidentally allowed to grow to a medium size (15–20 cm) (6–8 in). You simply dip slices of zucchini into water, then dust them in flour and fry in corn oil until they are golden and crisp.

3 medium zucchini (courgettes), cut into 1 cm (½ in) thick slices
sea salt
freshly ground black pepper

corn oil for frying
2 tablespoons plain (all purpose) flour
Aïoli (page 161), to serve

Dip the zucchini slices into cold water and dust lightly with salt, pepper and plain flour.

Heat 190 ml (6 ½ fl oz) corn oil in a frying pan until it starts to sizzle. Fry the zucchini slices, a few at a time, until golden and crisp. Remove them from the pan and drain briefly on kitchen paper. If the flour starts to burn in the oil after a few batches, tip out the oil and wipe the pan clean with kitchen paper. Start afresh with more corn oil, heating it well before frying the zucchini slices.

Serve the fried zucchini while hot with Aïoli.

Serves 6

Tomato, basil and black olive salad

This simple salad combines just four main ingredients: sweet tomatoes (and you really do need to use ripe and flavoursome summer tomatoes), salty olives, fragrant basil and nutty, herbaceous extra virgin olive oil. They combine to create the perfect salad.

I find that peeling the tomatoes enhances their sweetness. Greek basil works particularly well in this salad because it has tiny leaves that you can leave whole so they stay bright green without discolouring. If you can't find Greek basil, then use a large-leaf variety and tear the leaves into smaller pieces. The flavour will be the same, but the appearance will not be as good, because cutting or tearing the leaves will cause them to bruise and discolour somewhat.

3 ripe, sweet tomatoes
80 g (3 oz) kalamata olives
¼ cup Greek basil leaves

2 tablespoons extra virgin olive oil
salt
freshly ground black pepper

Bring a large saucepan of water to the boil. Cut a small cross in the base of each tomato and drop them carefully into the boiling water. Remove after 30 seconds and refresh immediately in iced water. This will make it easier to slip off the skins. Slice the tomatoes into wedges and place in a serving bowl.

Thoroughly wash the olives, and use a small, sharp knife to cut the flesh away from the pits in neat slices. Discard the pits.

Add the olive slices and basil leaves to the tomatoes. Drizzle with olive oil and sprinkle with salt and pepper. Toss together very gently and serve.

Serves 4

Mizuna salad with roasted pumpkin, pine nuts and ras-el-hanout dressing

In this salad, the sweet pumpkin (squash), peppery mizuna leaves and toasted pine nuts are perfectly balanced with the exotic spiciness of the dressing. It makes an ideal accompaniment to roast lamb.

½ Japanese pumpkin (kabocha squash), peeled and seeds removed
125 ml (4 fl oz) corn oil
salt
freshly ground black pepper
40 g (1 ½ oz) pine nuts
300 g (10 ½ oz) mixed rocket (arugula), mizuna and spinach leaves

Ras-el-hanout dressing
1 teaspoon cumin seeds
1 tablespoon cardamom pods
1 cinnamon stick
1 small nutmeg
1 teaspoon cloves
2 teaspoons white peppercorns
2 teaspoons black peppercorns
1 teaspoon cayenne pepper
190 ml (6 ½ fl oz) extra virgin olive oil
60 ml (2 fl oz) white wine vinegar

Preheat the oven to 220°C (430°F) and line a baking tray with baking paper.

Cut the pumpkin into 5 cm x 2 cm (2 in x ¾ in) pieces. Drizzle with corn oil and sprinkle generously with salt and pepper. Lay the pumpkin pieces flat on the baking tray and roast for about 45 minutes until golden brown and crisp around the edges. Remove from the oven and leave to cool.

Lower the oven temperature to 170°C (340°F). Scatter the pine nuts onto a small baking tray and roast for 7 minutes, or until they colour a light golden brown. Remove from the oven and leave to cool.

Wash the salad leaves well then pat dry.

To make the dressing toast the cumin seeds in a pan for two minutes over a low heat, until fragrant.

Break the cardamom pods open with a rolling pin or mortar and pestle, remove the seeds and discard the empty pods. Crumble the cinnamon stick, crush or grate the nutmeg, then grind all the spices in a spice grinder or mortar and pestle and combine.

Whisk oil and vinegar together, add 1 tablespoon of the mixed spice mix and whisk. Add salt to taste.

When ready to make the salad, combine the pumpkin and salad leaves in a large mixing bowl. Pour on the dressing and toss gently. Tip out onto a serving platter and pile the pine nuts on top.

Serves 6

Roasted beetroot salad with garlic and labne

Roasting beetroot (beets) really intensifies their flavour. As it cooks, the sweet juices run out onto the roasting tray and caramelise, and you do have to make sure that they don't burn. Beetroot can take a long time to cook, so I like to cover them with foil for the first 40 minutes. Then I remove the foil so that the outer edges roast properly in the heat. I always peel the beetroot before roasting them, so as not to lose the lovely caramelised exterior.

Labne is strained yoghurt, and its creamy flavour goes perfectly with the intense sweetness of the roasted beetroot and garlic.

salt
500 g (1 lb 2 oz) plain yoghurt
1 kg (2 lb 3 oz) medium beetroot (beets), peeled
125 ml (4 fl oz) corn oil
freshly ground black pepper

1 whole head garlic
1 tablespoon cumin seeds
120 ml (4 fl oz) extra virgin olive oil
40 ml (1¼ fl oz) red wine vinegar

Start making the labne the day before you wish to serve the salad. Stir 1 teaspoon of salt into the yoghurt and tip into a colander lined with a clean piece of muslin (cheesecloth). Sit the colander in a bowl and refrigerate for 24 hours. As the liquid drains away, the yoghurt will thicken into a firm, dense mass called labne. Use two soup spoons to form the labne into about 8 even-sized balls and place them on a lightly oiled plate. Refrigerate until ready to use.

Preheat the oven to 180°C (350°F) and lightly oil a small baking tray.

Arrange the beetroots in the baking tray. Drizzle with corn oil and sprinkle with salt and pepper. Cover the tray with foil and roast for 40 minutes. Remove the foil and continue roasting for another 50 minutes, or until the beetroots are easily pierced with a sharp knife. When cool enough to handle, slice the beetroots into wedges.

On another small baking tray, roast the head of garlic for 30 minutes, or until it is soft to the touch. When cool enough to handle, divide into individual cloves, peel and set aside.

Scatter the cumin seeds onto a small baking tray and roast for 7 minutes, or until fragrant.

Whisk the olive oil and vinegar together and season with salt and pepper.

Arrange the beetroot wedges in a large serving bowl and scatter on the roasted garlic cloves. Sit the labne balls on top and sprinkle them with the toasted cumin seeds. Drizzle over the dressing and serve.

Serves 4

Warm salad of silver beet, gorgonzola and walnuts

If you grew up in Australia in the 1950s and 1960s, as I did, you'll probably remember silver beet (Swiss chard) as a dull, waterlogged, boiled vegetable. Everyone grew it in their back yard so it was the most commonplace green vegetable on the Australian dinner table, along with boiled potatoes and carrots. It was not until many years later that I discovered just how delicious silver beet can be, especially when cooked with a little olive oil until just wilted, and then combined with the crunch of toasted walnuts, and tangy melted gorgonzola.

This is a lively, bold dish, complete in itself, or brilliant as a glossy accompaniment to a grilled (broiled) beef rib eye.

100 g (3½ oz) walnuts
1 bunch (about 8 large stalks) silver beet
   (Swiss chard)

2 tablespoons extra virgin olive oil
100 g (3½ oz) gorgonzola, cut into
   2 cm (¾ in) cubes

Preheat the oven to 180°C (350°F). Roast the walnuts for 10 minutes, or until a deep golden brown. Tip them into a tea (dish) towel and rub vigorously to loosen and remove the skins.

Cut the stems from the silver beet and discard them. Wash the leaves thoroughly and shake off excess moisture. Place them in a large saucepan with the oil over a medium heat. Cover the pan and cook for a few minutes until the leaves start to wilt. Remove the lid and add the walnuts and gorgonzola. Replace the lid and give the pan a bit of a shake. Cook for a few more minutes until the gorgonzola starts to melt and the silver beet has wilted.

Lift the silver beet out onto a serving plate and pour on the walnuts and the sauce which will have formed in the bottom of the pan.

Serves 4

Salad of seared scallops, grapefruit and avocado with a citrus–poppy seed dressing

The tangy grapefruit and citrus dressing works really well with the smooth blandness of avocado and rich sweetness of the scallops.

As with all seafood, try to buy local scallops for maximum freshness. Make sure they haven't been soaked in water. They should be a pale creamy colour with bright orange coral, and they shouldn't smell fishy.

Dressing
125 ml (4 fl oz) fresh orange juice
80 ml (3 fl oz) lemon juice
125 ml (4 fl oz) extra virgin olive oil
1 teaspoon poppy seeds

Salad
3 grapefruit (ruby if possible)
2 avocados
24 scallops, corals intact
30 g (1 oz) butter
salt
125 ml (4 fl oz) extra virgin olive oil

To make the dressing, combine the orange and lemon juices in a saucepan and bring to the boil. Simmer vigorously until reduced to a thick syrup. Remove from the heat and leave to cool. When cold, slowly whisk the oil into the citrus syrup until well combined. Stir in the poppy seeds.

Peel the grapefruit with a sharp knife, making sure that you remove all the pith. Carefully cut down the sides of the membranes between each segment of fruit, then flip the segments out.

Cut the avocados in half lengthwise. Remove the stones and peel away the skins. Cut into 1.5 cm slices. Place alternating slices of avocado and grapefruit on each of four serving plates, arranging them in the centre of the plate like spokes of a wheel.

Trim away the dark intestinal threads from the scallops, as well as any traces of brownish beard, but leave the corals intact. Melt the butter in a heavy-based frying pan until it begins to froth. Sprinkle the scallops lightly with salt and drizzle with the oil. Fry in batches for 3 minutes on each side, until they are starting to turn crisp and golden on the outside, but are still rare in the centre.

Divide the scallops among the serving plates, placing some on top of the salad and some around the edge of the plate. Drizzle on the dressing and serve straight away.

Serves 4

Braised broad beans with dill and green garlic Koukia

I have noticed that some Greek women pick broad (fava) beans when they are very young, while the pods are still small. They like to cook and eat them whole – pods, beans and all. I find the furry texture and flavour of the outer pods a little unpleasant, so I prefer to wait until the beans have grown a bit larger and to remove them from their pods before cooking.

You can add a couple of globe artichokes to this dish, which add a delicious flavour. But make sure you use fresh artichokes, not pickled or preserved ones that don't have the same flavour.

1 kg young broad (fava) beans
2–3 globe artichokes (optional)
1 onion, diced
2 stalks green garlic or four cloves garlic, chopped
½ cup chopped dill
190 ml (6 ½ fl oz) extra virgin olive oil

80 ml (3 fl oz) water
salt
freshly ground black pepper
plain yoghurt to serve

Pod the beans and place them in a saucepan. If there are some older, large, tough-looking ones, you may need to trim the end off where there is a little lip. (I do not recommend double peeling the beans for this recipe, as they may break up as they cook and become too mushy.)

If using artichokes, peel the stalks and trim away the tough outer leaves. Slice across the top half of the artichokes and discard the pointy bits. You should be left with goblet-shaped artichokes, with the stalks still attached. Slice them in half lengthways which will reveal the inner hairy choke. Use the point of a sharp knife to remove all the hairs. Immediately transfer the artichokes to a bowl of water acidulated with lemon juice to prevent them from discolouring.

Add the artichokes (if using), onion, garlic, dill, olive oil and water to the pan with the beans and season with salt and pepper. Cover the pan and bring to the boil over a moderate heat. Cook for about 30 minutes, or until the beans are tender. Remove from the heat and leave to cool a little before serving with a generous dollop of plain yoghurt.

Serves 4

Green beans with tomato, garlic, onion and parsley Fassolakia

This is a classic Greek summer lunch dish and we enjoy some variation of it at least a couple of times a week. You can eat it warm, at room temperature, or cold as a salad. This dish does use quite a lot of olive oil, so don't be faint-hearted. It should not be watery, so cook until most of the liquid from the vegetables has evaporated and the tomatoes have combined with the oil to make a delicious thick sauce.

1 kg (2 lb 3 oz) green beans, topped and tailed
1 onion, diced
3 cloves garlic, chopped
1 cup flat-leaf (Italian) parsley
4 ripe tomatoes
2 teaspoons tomato paste (concentrated purée) dissolved in 125 ml (4 fl oz) water

190 ml (6 ½ fl oz) extra virgin olive oil
salt
freshly ground black pepper
slices of feta cheese to serve
fresh crusty bread to serve

Place the beans, onion, garlic and parsley in a large saucepan. Cut the tomatoes in half crosswise and grate the flesh coarsely into the saucepan, discarding the skins. Pour in the tomato paste mixture and the oil and season with salt and pepper. Sit a plate on top of the vegetables then cover the pan with a lid and bring to the boil. Cook for 15 minutes, then lower the heat and simmer for 30 minutes.

Serve with slices of feta cheese and fresh crusty bread.

Serves 6

Summer vegetable casserole Tourlou

Tourlou is a dish that has evolved using the abundant produce from Greek village vegetable gardens in the summer, and the cook uses whatever is available. Use as many or as few vegetables as you like and don't be tempted to add water. The vegetables will give off liquid as they cook, which will combine with the oil to make the sauce.

1 eggplant (aubergine)
salt
300 g (10 ½ oz) okra (if available)
125 ml (4 fl oz) vinegar
2 onions, finely sliced
3 cloves garlic, finely chopped
1 zucchini (courgette), cut into 4 cm (1 ½ in) dice
1 red capsicum (pepper) or 2 long yellow wax
    peppers, cut into 4 cm (1 ½ in) dice
500 g (1 lb 2 oz) green beans, topped and tailed

2 potatoes, quartered
1 cup flat-leaf (Italian) parsley leaves, finely
    chopped
3 ripe tomatoes, halved and coarsely grated,
    skins discarded
190 ml (6 ½ fl oz) extra virgin olive oil
freshly ground black pepper
slices of feta cheese to serve
fresh crusty bread to serve

Cut the eggplant into 2 cm (¾ in) cubes, sprinkle with salt and sit in a colander. Use a sharp knife to cut around the tops of the okra to remove the rough parts and make a little pointy cap. Sprinkle with vinegar and sit in a colander. Set the eggplant and okra aside while you prepare the remaining vegetables. Rinse thoroughly and pat dry before using.

Layer the vegetables in a heavy-based pot, starting with the onions, then followed by the eggplant, garlic, zucchini, capsicums, beans, potatoes, okra, parsley and tomato pulp. Make sure the potatoes and okra go on the top as they tend to break up if you put them in the bottom of the pot, and the whole dish becomes mushy.

Pour on the olive oil and season with salt and pepper. Cover the saucepan and bring to the boil over a medium heat. Cook for 20 minutes, then lower the heat and simmer for 20 minutes. Leave to cool a little before serving with slices of feta cheese and fresh crusty bread.

Serves 6

Baked eggplant stuffed with tomato, garlic, onion and parsley Imam bayaldi

This is a very popular summer dish in Greece, even though its origins are undoubtedly Turkish.

Imam bayaldi translates to 'the fainting Imam' and there are a number of different explanations for the name. The most widely accepted is that the Imam (a Muslim priest) married the daughter of a rich oil merchant, whose dowry was twelve bottles of the highest quality olive oil. For the first twelve nights of their married life she prepared eggplant (aubergine) stuffed with tomato, garlic, onion and parsley and braised in the olive oil. On the thirteenth night, no such dish graced their dinner table. When informed that there was no olive oil left, the Imam fainted.

....

4 medium eggplants (aubergines)
salt
125 ml (4 fl oz) extra virgin olive oil
2 onions, sliced
3 cloves garlic, finely chopped

1 cup flat-leaf (Italian) parsley leaves, chopped
4 large ripe tomatoes, diced
freshly ground black pepper
250 ml (8 ½ fl oz) vegetable oil

Preheat the oven to 180°C (350°F).

Cut the eggplants in half lengthwise and make a long incision down through the flesh of each half. Sprinkle with salt and leave for half an hour. Rinse thoroughly and dry with a tea (dish) towel.

Heat the oil in a large frying pan. Add the onion and sauté until soft and golden. Add the garlic and parsley and cook for another minute. Add the tomatoes and season with salt and pepper. Cook for 5 minutes then remove from the heat.

In another large frying pan, heat the vegetable oil and fry the eggplants on both sides, until the cut side is golden brown. Drain on kitchen paper.

Arrange the eggplants in a baking tray, cut side up, and fill the cavities generously with the tomato filling. Bake for 1 hour or until soft. Allow to cool before serving.

Serves 4

ABOVE *Clockwise from centre, Baked Eggplant Stuffed with Tomato, Garlic, Onion and Parsley; Green Beans with Tomato, Onion and Parsley; Summer Vegetable Casserole.*

Kosta

Kosta arrived in Australia in 1974. Having just completed his compulsory military service in Greece, he was beckoned to Australia to help his older brother Chris, whose restaurant in Lorne was experiencing huge success. The brothers soon thought of opening another restaurant and Chris helped Kosta to set up at the other end of the main street. Kosta was an expert grill cook so they decided to capitalise on that and called the restaurant The Steak House.

Kosta and I met at the Continental hotel in Melbourne, one winter's night in 1977 when I went there for a drink with friends after a mid-year exam. I was studying law at Melbourne University and was in my final year. Kosta was soon coming around to my house with gifts of beautifully wrapped boxes of Greek cakes, gratefully received and consumed. I was trying to stay focused on my studies but found it almost impossible to resist the cheeky, reckless, handsome boy always wanting me to go to Greek nightclubs. It was all a world away from my conservative Anglo-Saxon upbringing.

That summer we moved to Lorne and together we re-opened the restaurant and the newly named Kostas Taverna took off from there. Kosta cooked the steaks and I waited on tables. It was all terribly unprofessional; friends who came to stay were recruited to help either as waiters or kitchen hands and we opened and closed as and when we felt like it.

We learnt as we went and business picked up. I started helping in the kitchen and was soon cooking alongside Kosta. I was working as a solicitor during the week and as a cook on the weekend, but before long Kosta was running the dining room and I took over the realm of the kitchen full-time.

Kosta has charisma; he is able to talk to all people and make each one feel special. I have come across so many people and heard reference to many others who think that they are Kosta's

best friend. It seems that he is able to make each person feel that they have entered into a realm of friendship, a special bond. He seemingly never gets bored listening to people and can stay in the restaurant talking to customers, sharing a bottle of wine or a beer until late every night. This amazing stamina is a characteristic shared by many other Greeks in business who spend from early morning till last thing at night in their shops, day after day.

Kosta's greatest strength — apart from cooking the perfect steak and grilling a fish like no-one else could — has always been in buying. He never tires of seeking out the freshest and best available product. In those early days he would drive to Geelong many days of the week to to be at the fisheries when the boats came in and pick the best quality fish. He would come home beaming with special treats: a barbouni for me and some fresh flounders for the boys.

Seeking out specialty suppliers in Melbourne was another favourite past-time. Kosta knew every Greek, Italian and Mediterranean wholesaler. At least once a week we made the trip to Melbourne, coming home with a truck full of Greek extra virgin olive oil, feta, kalamata olives, salt cod, bags of fresh coffee beans, parmigiano reggiano, wine vinegars, saffron, Greek newspapers and all sorts of things that were unattainable in a small country town. It was like shopping for a party, and to this day it has never lost its thrill.

Fish and seafood

The Greeks are a fish-eating people. They know the value of eating seafood regularly for both nutritional and monetary reasons, as it has always been affordable in a country made up of thousands of islands, while the scarcity of available grassland for grazing animals has made meat a luxury. Fresh fish is delivered to most villages at least twice a week, and on other days it can be purchased from a market in a village nearby. It is transported in the back of a van or utility truck and displayed in boxes of ice. Gypsy music blares out from loud speakers and sets of old-fashioned scales swing from the back. The fishmonger stops on every corner to call out his wares. 'Fresca psaria! Sardella! Bakalao! Kolious!'

Seafood has always been a significant component of the menu at both Kostas and A la Grecque, and Kosta goes to any lengths to make sure we have a good selection. He does the rounds of all the local suppliers every day, seeking out the best available fish and procuring it by any means.

During the years that I worked as a solicitor in Geelong, Yiayia and Papou came to Australia in the summer months to mind the children. Kosta would go down to the Geelong port in the morning to buy fish. There was a tiny tin shed on the wharf where a couple of derelict looking old men with stubbly chins, wearing army great coats, watching TV stubby in hand, cigarette stuck to the lip would sell whatever fish they had caught that day. Unnamed, uncleaned, wrapped in newspaper. Their only customers were Europeans. Sadly, these characters were moved on in the name of progress.

In those days nobody wanted the octopus, which was caught as a by-product in the crayfish pots at Lorne. The fishermen gave it away or sold it for fifty cents a kilo. It was not something which Australians were familiar with preparing or eating. But to Greeks, octopus is as valuable as crayfish. The flavour is rich and the meaty texture of the flesh makes it versatile. It is ideal for cooking over charcoals; it can be braised as stifado, pickled with vinegar and made into a salad, or boiled with potatoes, onions and carrots in a casserole.

Kalamari and cuttlefish were unheard of in Australian restaurants until the 1970s. They were used only as bait for catching other fish until the migrants from the Mediterranean introduced them to the dining tables in their restaurants. Fried kalamari has been our most popular dish at both Kostas and A la Grecque. We can never get enough fresh local kalamari to keep up with the demand in the summertime. Quickly fried at a high temperature in good quality oil, it is always tasty and needs only a little tzatziki or aïoli to balance the sweet flavour and fried texture.

Some fish may be suited to cooking in the oven or being made into a soup, but otherwise a fresh piece of fish should be presented as simply as possible to reveal its true flavour. To this end, most fish is pan-fried or cooked over charcoals, drizzled with latholemono (olive oil, lemon juice and seasonings) and served with a simple salad or vegetable dishes and bread.

Pan-fried fish

Pan-frying is a suitable method for cooking most fish, but remember that the cooking time and temperature will depend on the size and thickness of the fillet. King George whiting fillets, for instance, will cook much more quickly than blue eye.

1 x 240 g (8 ½ oz) fish fillet (e.g. blue eye, snapper, flathead, John Dory or King George whiting, flounder, porgy or bream)

salt
2 tablespoons corn or olive oil
freshly ground black pepper

Season the fish lightly with salt. Heat the oil in a heavy-based frying pan until just smoking. Carefully place the fish in the pan, skin side down – the oil will sizzle. Fry on a high heat for 1–2 minutes so the skin crisps and colours golden brown. Lower the heat to medium–high and fry for 4 minutes. Turn the fish carefully and fry for a further 4–5 minutes. You only need to turn the fish once. Don't fiddle with it or you won't achieve a crisp, golden crust. To see if the fish is cooked, insert the point of a sharp knife into the thickest part of the fish; the flesh should be white and not translucent. Season to taste and serve piping hot from the pan.

Serves 1

Chargrilled sardines on toasted sourdough

Chargrilling over coals, wood or gas on a barbecue is a particularly good method for oily fish such as salmon, mackerel, sardines or tuna. As with other cooking methods, the time will vary, depending on the thickness of the fish. Sardines and small mackerel will take about 5 minutes on each side. Larger fish, such as tuna or salmon, will take 5–6 minutes for medium-rare. You should aim for a well-coloured crisp outer crust.

Make sure your grill is very clean, to prevent the fish from sticking. Before you start cooking, clean the grill bars thoroughly, then rub them lightly with kitchen paper and olive oil to leave a fine film that won't catch alight on the flames.

Light your barbecue, and if you're using solid fuel, let the fire burn until the flames have died down and you are left with glowing embers. I find fish is easy to cook if you use a fold-over metal fish basket (called a skara). Make sure it sits about 15 cm (6 in) above the coals.

6–8 small fresh sardines, cleaned
extra virgin olive oil
sea salt flakes

freshly ground black pepper
few slices sourdough bread
2 cloves garlic

Brush the fish lightly with oil and sprinkle with salt. Arrange them in the fish basket and cook over glowing embers for 4–5 minutes. Turn over and cook for another 4–5 minutes.

While the fish are cooking, place the slices of bread on the barbecue and cook on both sides until golden brown. Rub generously with garlic then drizzle liberally with oil and season with salt flakes and pepper. Top with the chargrilled sardines and eat while hot with Latholemono (page 160).

Serves 1

Sardines baked in the oven

Fresh sardines are abundant in Greece, especially in the spring when they are plump. Because they are an oily fish they are particularly good for you. Just as importantly, they are very tasty. When we are in Greece we eat them almost every night, cooked on the barbecue, lightly pan-fried or baked in the oven.

800 g (1 lb 12 oz) fresh sardines
salt
freshly ground black pepper
½ cup flat-leaf (Italian) parsley leaves,
    finely chopped

juice of 2 lemons
125 ml (4 fl oz) extra virgin olive oil
125 ml (4 fl oz) water

Preheat the oven to 200°C (400°F).

Clean the sardines by inserting your thumb and finger into the gill cavity and pulling the gills out. This will pull away the guts as well. Rub your fingers along the fish from tail to head, to remove any little scales. Leave the heads attached.

Sprinkle the sardines lightly with salt and pepper and place them in a small baking tray or oven dish. Sprinkle on the chopped parsley. Mix the lemon juice with the oil and water and pour over the sardines. Place in the oven and bake for 20–25 minutes.

Serve straight away with a crisp lettuce salad.

Serves 4

Oven-baked flathead with potatoes, tomatoes and onion

In my view, flathead fillets and sardines are both particularly well suited to baking in the oven. But make sure you ask your fishmonger for rock flathead, not tiger flathead, which is a quite different fish. Rock flathead is great for almost any method of cooking. It has a sweet flavour and a firm texture, so it's easy to cook without drying out and falling to pieces or sticking. It's ideal for oven-baking as it retains moisture much better than more delicate fish such as whiting.

8 medium flathead or flounder fillets
2 onions, sliced
4 large potatoes, peeled and cut into wedges
3 cloves garlic, roughly chopped
3 large ripe tomatoes, cut into wedges

125 ml (4 fl oz) extra virgin olive oil
salt
freshly ground black pepper
½ cup flat-leaf (Italian) parsley leaves, roughly
   chopped

Ask your fishmonger to trim the flathead fillets and to remove the bones from the upper body cavities.

Preheat the oven to 200°C (400°F) and lightly oil a baking tray.

Layer the onions on the bottom of the baking tray. Arrange the potatoes on top and scatter on the garlic. Place the tomatoes on top and drizzle with half the oil. Season liberally with salt and pepper and place in the oven for 45–50 minutes until the potatoes are starting to crisp up around the edges.

Season the fish fillets lightly with salt. Tuck the fish in among the vegetables. Drizzle with the rest of the oil and scatter on the parsley. Return to the oven and bake for 20 minutes, or until the fish is just cooked through.

Serves 4

Mussels with rice and dill

Kosta's mother would often make this dish for lunch. Our boys loved it when they were young as it's best eaten with the fingers, using the mussel shells to scoop up the rice. I have seen Turkish recipes that include currants and pine nuts, but I think it's great with just the flavours of the mussels and dill.

500 ml (17 fl oz) Fish Stock (page 27)
800 g (1 lb 12 oz) mussels, scrubbed clean and beards removed
125 ml (4 fl oz) white wine
2 tablespoons extra virgin olive oil
10 spring onions (scallions), finely chopped
1 clove garlic, finely chopped

320 g (11½ oz) medium grain white rice, well rinsed under cold running water
125 ml (4 fl oz) reserved mussel cooking liquid (see method)
½ cup dill, chopped
freshly ground black pepper

Heat the stock in a saucepan until it reaches boiling point.

Put the mussels and wine into a large saucepan with a tight-fitting lid. Cook over a low–medium heat, shaking the pan gently from time to time. Check after 4 minutes and discard any mussels that haven't opened. Tip into a colander and reserve the cooking liquid. Strain this liquid through a clean piece of muslin (cheesecloth) to remove any sand or grit. Set the mussels aside.

Rinse out the saucepan and add the oil. Heat gently and sauté the spring onions and garlic until they start to soften. Add the rice and stir well. Pour on the boiling stock and the reserved mussel cooking liquid and lower the heat to gentle simmer. Cover the saucepan and cook for about 10 minutes until nearly all the liquid has been absorbed by the rice. Scatter in the dill and season with pepper. Do not add any salt as the mussel liquid will be quite salty.

Add the mussels, shells and all, to the saucepan. Use a large kitchen spoon to stir everything around, so that the rice goes right into the mussel shells. Cook for another 2–3 minutes. Ladle into deep bowls and serve.

Serves 4

Salmon with mussels, fennel and saffron

This dish was inspired by one I enjoyed many years ago, at a restaurant in New York. Although it wasn't a Greek restaurant, it had a Greek name, Zoë (which means 'life'). I don't know if the restaurant still exists, but it lives on in my memory, and in my version of the dish.

400 g (14 oz) mussels, scrubbed clean and beards removed
125 ml (4 fl oz) white wine
80 ml (3 fl oz) extra virgin olive oil
4 x 250 g (9 oz) Tasmanian salmon fillets
30 g (1 oz) butter

2 golden shallots, peeled and finely sliced
½ bulb fennel, finely sliced
20 strands saffron
250 ml (8 ½ fl oz) Fish Stock (page 27)
125 ml (4 fl oz) reserved mussel cooking liquid (see method)

Put the mussels and white wine into a large saucepan with a tight-fitting lid. Cook over a low–medium heat, shaking the pan gently from time to time. Check after 4 minutes and discard any mussels that haven't opened. Tip into a colander and reserve the cooking liquid. Strain this liquid through a clean piece of muslin (cheesecloth) to remove any sand or grit. Set the mussels aside.

Reserve about 12 mussels to serve in their shells as garnish. Remove the mussel meat from the remaining shells.

Heat the oil in a heavy-based frying pan. Fry the salmon over a fairly high heat for about 4 minutes on each side, or until golden on the outside but still rare inside. Carefully transfer the salmon to a plate.

Lower the heat and add the butter to the pan. Sauté the shallots and fennel for a few minutes until the fennel is soft. Add the saffron, fish stock and reserved mussel cooking liquid. Bring to the boil, then lower the heat and simmer until the liquid is reduced by half.

Return the salmon to the pan together with the reserved mussel meat. Cook for a few minutes until just warmed through. Be careful not to overcook or the mussels will be rubbery. The salmon should be no more than medium-rare.

Serve in shallow bowls, distributing the mussels evenly around each piece of salmon. Garnish with the reserved mussels in their shells and ladle on the hot cooking liquid.

Serves 4

Deep-fried kalamari

When buying kalamari, make sure that you're actually getting kalamari and not arrow squid. On kalamari, the side wings extend the whole length along either side of the body. On arrow squid, the wings are just little triangles at the bottom tip of the body that form a dart shape.

Always choose kalamari that are a whitish-grey colour, speckled with a little black ink. They should not be pink. Kalamari should always smell clean, not fishy or of ammonia. When cleaning and preparing kalamari take care with the ink sac as it is quite delicate and it may burst and squirt ink all over you. Don't worry if some ink gets on the kalamari as it is quite tasty. In fact some recipes for braising even require the ink to be added.

To clean kalamari, first pull the head and tentacles away from the body and set them aside. Insert your fingers into the body cavity and pull out the guts and the thin, transparent cartilage, which looks like a piece of plastic. Now slide your fingertips under the blackish membrane that covers the body and peel it away. Rinse the body inside and out then pat it dry. Cut into strips or into 1.5 cm (¾ in) rings.

Pinch your thumb and forefinger nails in between the eyes and the tentacles and separate them. Alternatively, use a knife to cut the tentacles away from the head. Use your thumbs to pop the beak out from the centre of the tentacles. Discard the beak, head and ink sac and keep the tentacles. Rinse and pat dry then cut them into 7 cm (2¾ in) lengths.

....

6 medium kalamari
150 g (5½ oz) plain (all-purpose) flour
1 teaspoon salt

1 teaspoon freshly ground black pepper
corn oil or sunflower oil, for frying
1 teaspoon dried oregano

Clean and prepare the kalamari as described above. Mix the flour with the salt and pepper. Dip the kalamari pieces into the seasoned flour, shaking off excess.

Pour the oil into a heavy-based saucepan to a depth of about 2 cm (¾ in). Heat until smoking, which is about 220°C (430°F) if you have a thermometer. Carefully drop the kalamari into the oil, a few pieces at a time. Be careful not to overcrowd the pan or the temperature will drop and you will not achieve a crisp, golden crust. Drain briefly on kitchen paper and sprinkle on a little dried oregano. Serve with green salad and Aïoli (page 161) or Tzatziki (page 47).

Serves 6

Salt cod and potatoes cooked in milk

This recipe is inspired by one in *Honey from a Weed*, by Patience Gray, which is a timeless book of stories about cooking and eating in Italy and Greece. The Greeks call salt cod or ling 'bakalao'. It is generally eaten in winter when fresh fish and vegetables may be scarce.

In her recipe, Patience Gray recommends using whole olives as she says that pitted olives can stain the pale colour of the dish. If you use whole olives you need to be careful as they can be tooth-breakers for the unsuspecting diner!

1 kg (2 lb 3 oz) salt cod or ling
1–2 bay leaves
2 tablespoons extra virgin olive oil
1 large onion, sliced
6 potatoes, cut into 1 cm (½ in) slices
a few sprigs fresh oregano
freshly ground white pepper
500 ml (17 fl oz) milk

125 ml (4 fl oz) cream (whipping)
½ teaspoon fresh ground nutmeg
1 clove garlic, finely chopped
finely chopped parsley leaves
a little chilli oil
2 hard-boiled eggs, sliced
12 black olives

Soak the salt cod in cold water in the refrigerator for 24 hours, changing the water three times. Drain well and cut the fish into portions. Put the cod into a saucepan and cover with plenty of cold water. Add the bay leaves and bring very slowly to a gentle simmer. Do not let the water boil, or the fish will become tough. Simmer for 5 minutes then remove from the heat and leave to stand for an hour. Drain off the water. Remove the skin and bones and flake the fish.

Heat the oil in a cast iron or heavy-based casserole dish. Arrange a layer of sliced onions and potatoes in the base of the dish and top with a layer of flaked fish. Repeat to create another layer then sprinkle with oregano and season with pepper. Pour on the milk and cream and bring to a simmer over a medium heat. Simmer for about 20 minutes or until the potatoes are cooked. By this time, most of the liquid will have been absorbed and what remains will be rather creamy.

Sprinkle on the nutmeg, garlic and parsley. Add a few drops of chilli oil and cook for a few more minutes. Top with slices of hard-boiled egg and scatter on the olives just before serving.

Serves 4

Prawns with okra Garithes me bamyies

Okra is a popular vegetable in Greece where almost everyone grows it in the garden. The plant belongs to the mallow family. It has a beautiful flower and the fruits grow very quickly – from tiny to overgrown, seemingly overnight. Okra are best picked when they're about 7–8 cm (2¾–3¼ in), but like zucchinis (courgettes), they seem to hide beneath the leaves and you need to pick them every day or risk them turning into giants. The best time to pick okra is early in the morning, and you need to wear long sleeves as the leaves are covered with tiny, prickly hairs that can irritate the skin.

In this dish the prawns (shrimp) and okra are cooked separately and then served together. The okra have a soft texture when they are cooked, and the prawns need to be fried on quite a high heat until they are just cooked through, but crisp and golden on the outside.

500 g (1 lb 2 oz) okra
125 ml (4 fl oz) vinegar
1 onion, sliced
3 cloves garlic, finely chopped
2 ripe tomatoes, halved and coarsely grated, skins discarded

125 ml (4 fl oz) extra virgin olive oil
½ cup chopped parsley or coriander (cilantro) leaves
salt
freshly ground black pepper
12 green prawns (shrimp), shelled and deveined
2 tablespoons corn oil

Use a sharp knife to cut around the tops of the okra to remove the rough parts and make a little pointy cap. Sprinkle with vinegar and sit in a colander for 10 minutes. Rinse thoroughly and pat dry before using.

Place the okra in a saucepan with the sliced onion and garlic. Add the tomato pulp, followed by the olive oil, herbs, ½ teaspoon salt and pepper. Cover the pan with a lid and cook over a low heat for 30 minutes. The okra should be soft, but not disintegrating.

Sprinkle the prawns with salt. Heat the corn oil in a frying pan. Add the prawns and sauté on a medium–high heat for 2 minutes on each side until pink and starting to turn crisp and golden brown.

Serve the okra in a shallow bowl and arrange the prawns on top.

Serves 4

Octopus stifado

A stifado is a slow-cooked casserole made with a large amount of onions in a tomato sauce. It is often made with rabbit or hare, using tiny pickling onions. Peeling and preparing these little onions is extremely time-consuming and fiddly, so instead I often use golden shallots, which have a lovely delicate onion flavour, or immature red (Spanish) onions (these look like large spring onions/scallions, with 3–4 cm (1 ¼–1 ½ in) reddish bulbs). Both these types of onion are available in produce markets in the spring.

Octopus makes a great stifado as the juices released during the long, slow cooking combine with the tomato and shallots to make a rich sauce.

1–2 kg (2 lb 3 oz–4 lb 6 oz) octopus
30 golden shallots
190 ml (6 ½ fl oz) extra virgin olive oil
3 cloves garlic, sliced
2 potatoes, peeled and quartered
1 teaspoon salt

½ teaspoon freshly ground black pepper
3 ripe tomatoes, halved and coarsely grated,
  skins discarded
½ cup parsley leaves
1 bay leaf

Clean the octopus as described on page 64. Cut the body and tentacles into 10 cm (4 in) pieces.

Peel the shallots, leaving as much of the base intact as you can to prevent them from disintegrating as they cook.

Heat the oil in a heavy-based saucepan. Add the shallots and sauté until they begin to soften and turn a light golden brown. Stir in the garlic then add the potatoes and octopus pieces and season with salt and pepper. Add the tomato pulp and herbs and stir everything together well.

Cover the pan with a tight-fitting lid and bring to the boil. Lower the heat and simmer gently for 1–1½ hours, until the octopus is tender and the sauce is thick and rich.

Serves 6

Cuttlefish braised with red wine, tomato and garlic

Like kalamari and squid, cuttlefish is a cephalopod – a mollusc without a shell. It has a similar shaped body and eight tentacles covered with suckers emerging from the head. Like most cephalopods, cuttlefish have an ink sac, and squirt a cloud of black ink to help them escape from predators. But whereas kalamari and squid have an internal transparent cartilage, cuttlefish have an internal flat calciferous bone.

Cuttlefish flesh is a bit thicker and meatier than kalamari and squid, but it has a very similar flavour. Because it is fairly tough, it is particularly well suited to long, slow braising to tenderise the flesh.

To clean cuttlefish, pull the head and tentacles away from the body and set them aside. Slide your fingertips under the blackish membrane that covers the body and peel it away. Cut open the body and detach and discard the ink sac and guts. Remove the cuttlebone and discard it. Rinse the body inside and out then pat it dry. Cut into squares about 6 cm (2 ½ in). Remove the beak and discard it with the head. Cut the tentacles into thirds.

1 kg (2 lb 3 oz) cuttlefish
190 ml (6 ½ fl oz) extra virgin olive oil
3 red (Spanish) onions or 10 red spring onions, sliced
6 cloves garlic, chopped
1 cup parsley, chopped
250 ml (8 ½ fl oz) red wine

2 ripe tomatoes, halved and coarsely grated, skins discarded
2 teaspoons tomato paste (concentrated purée), dissolved in 2 tablespoons boiling water
½ teaspoon salt
freshly ground black pepper

Clean the cuttlefish as described above.

Heat the oil in a large heavy-based saucepan. Fry the cuttlefish in batches then transfer to a bowl and set aside. Keep the heat high and be careful not to overcrowd the pan or the cuttlefish will boil, rather than fry.

When all the cuttlefish is cooked, add the onions to the pan and sauté in the same oil, adding a little more if need be. Sauté until soft and golden, stirring to prevent them from sticking to the base of the pan. Add the garlic and parsley and stir everything together well. Add the wine then return the cuttlefish to the pan. Add the tomato pulp and paste and season with salt and pepper. Bring to the boil, then lower the heat and cover the pan with a lid. Simmer for 2 hours. The onions and garlic will melt into the tomatoes to create a thick, rich sauce. Serve in shallow bowls with crusty bread.

Serves 6

Connected to the land

Greek people maintain very strong family ties, which in most cases bind them to a village somewhere. Almost all Greeks have family members who live in a village. The family home or farm is hardly ever sold when parents die, but will be kept at all costs as a matter of pride, thus continuing the age-old connection of the Greek to the land. City dwellers make weekend trips to visit parents or to maintain their own small weekend houses and vegetable gardens. They return to their city apartments with a car load of home-grown vegetables, eggs, cheese and meat.

In Greece, many village households keep a couple of sheep or goats, or a dairy cow for their personal use, and nearly everyone has a few chickens, ducks or turkeys. These are not fancy breeds to be admired or bred for shows; they are there to provide eggs and meat for the table. Live birds are sold at markets everywhere and from the back of vans as they do the rounds of the villages. On our first nights back at our village house we have to get used to the sound of the roosters, whose crowing in the night soon becomes a comforting background noise to sweet dreams.

While we are in Greece we have daily constitutional walks to the next village, and we often run into Mitso grazing his animals. Mitso spent all of his working life toiling in a factory in Germany, but he always had a dream of returning to Greece. When he retired, he returned to his father's land to build his dream-house and keep a herd of sheep and goats. He has a flock of about fifteen animals that he takes out every morning and night to graze along the river flats, the verges of the roads and, after harvest, in among the wheat stubble. He never gets bored with leaning on his crook, watching and waiting for them to eat their fill.

Kosta and I often wonder how he can bring himself to kill and eat his animals after keeping such close company with them. But he seems able to detach his emotions and not feel any sentimentality toward them. It's an attitude shared by many older Greek people, which I believe to be the consequence of having known hunger and extreme poverty during the Second World War and the Greek Civil War. Animals are bred and kept to provide milk and meat, and not as pets to be indulged or enjoyed, which would be an inconceivable extravagance in the minds of that generation.

Although Kosta and I cannot keep poultry in Greece (as we are not there throughout the year to care for them) we do breed our own poultry at our home in Lorne. This means that we are both very aware that a lack of sentimentality is something that all farmers and small-holders have to learn. Ironically, it has come more easily to me than to Kosta. Having grown up on a farm, I know from first-hand experience that the meat on our tables comes as the result of an animal being slaughtered. Someone has to do this job and it must be carried out in the

quickest, most humane way possible. It is a part of the natural cycle of life, and eating healthy nutritious food starts with that connection to the land.

So I am the one who has the unenviable task of killing and dressing a bird for the pot.

We always have a flock of roosters fattening for the dinner table, but it has taken a great deal of persuasion to get Kosta to eat our home-grown birds. At first, he balked at the idea, but by cooking them in a soup or as a casserole with kritharaki, so he can't actually see the shape of the bird, I have been gradually able to convince him to eat them and to appreciate the flavour and value of a totally organic free-range bird. He now proudly invites friends to dinner to share a pot-roasted rooster with fennel and leeks from the garden.

....

Meat and poultry

Greece is traditionally a nation of farmers and fishermen and the Greek economy still relies heavily on agriculture. Greece became a member of the European Union in 1981 and since then the standard of living has improved substantially, particularly in rural areas, which have benefited from secure markets for their produce and generous subsidies for agricultural production.

Meat is still an expensive item however, as most of the arable land is used for crops, rather than grazing animals. There are no large cattle stations to supply beef cattle to the market as there are in Australia. Pigs are farmed commercially, as are chickens, and both are regularly consumed as the most affordable meat. Many villagers keep rabbits in a hutch in the back yard for personal consumption or they'll have a couple of sheep or goats, or a dairy cow also for their personal use. Some imported meat, such as Australian and New Zealand lamb, is available in city markets, but in village butcher shops, lamb and goat are not always available and most of the beef is of a lesser quality.

Feast days are always celebrated with meat. A whole spring lamb cooked on the spit is obligatory at Easter, roast pork or turkey are served at Christmas, and after church on Sundays there is always meat on the table, usually a beef pot roast consisting of beef stewed with potatoes or kokinisto, which has the addition of tomatoes.

Anyone who has travelled to Greece will know that most tavernas offer a limited range of meat dishes – such as chops, keftethes, souvlaki, or pork ribs – that are grilled over charcoal. Less expensive cuts of meat and fat are used in take-away shops to make the famous gyro (from the word 'gyrizo', meaning to turn in a circle). Souvlaki, one of the most famous Greek meat dishes, can also be made from cheaper cuts of pork, diced small and threaded onto a skewer, then cooked quickly over charcoals. For a more elegant dish, souvlaki can also be made from good quality lamb backstraps, marinated in herbs and olive oil.

Prime cuts are particularly expensive, though, so Greeks have a wide repertoire of dishes for tougher secondary cuts. They are often minced (ground) finely and made into keftethes, or combined with rice and herbs as a stuffing for zucchinis (courgettes), tomatoes or capsicums (peppers). Some cuts are ideally suited for slow-cooking. A piece of beef topside might be pot-roasted, pork shoulder combines beautifully with honeyed quinces in the autumn, and in the heat of the summer a free-range chicken or rooster can be made into casserole with lots of capsicums and tomatoes from the garden.

In Greece, every part of the animal is eaten, from a pig's head and trotters to beef cheeks and lamb's lungs. Offal (variety meat) is made into a fricassée with spring herbs and greens, and sheep's heads are often seen still connected to the carcass as it turns on a spit, and are picked over as a delicacy.

Nowadays all Greek village kitchens are well-equipped with ovens, but not long ago it was a common sight to see trays of meat and vegetables carried through the streets to the local bakery for roasting. They were carried home again afterwards when they were cool enough to hold, and this, I imagine, is the reason why Greeks generally prefer to eat their food at room temperature rather than very hot. It also allowed time to rest the meat and for flavours to develop.

Braised pork shoulder with quinces

Pork and quinces are a magical combination. When making this dish I cook the quinces first, usually the day before, using Stephanie Alexander's recipe for baked quinces with honey from her book *Feasts and Stories*. Even though that is a dessert recipe, I find that the quinces are not too sweet when combined with the pork. I usually cook a large quantity and use a few of them for the pork casserole. I keep the rest of the quinces in the fridge to eat with cream or vanilla ice cream or I'll use them in a tart, a pudding or a cake. They go with everything.

3 quinces
120 g (4 oz) unsalted butter
1½ tablespoons honey
125 ml (4 fl oz) water
1 kg (2 lb 3 oz) pork shoulder
salt

freshly ground black pepper
125 ml (4 fl oz) extra virgin olive oil
1 onion, finely sliced
2 cloves garlic, chopped
125 ml (4 fl oz) white wine or verjuice
1 small sprig of rosemary

Heat the oven to 160°C (320°F).

Wash the quinces well to remove any down from the skins. Cut them in half lengthwise and top and tail them. Remove the core to create a neat hollow – I find it easiest to use a melon baller – then arrange the quince halves in a baking dish, cut sides up. Place a small knob of butter and ½ tablespoon of honey in each cavity. Pour in the water and cover the dish with foil. Bake for 3 hours until the quinces are a deep pinky-red and very tender.

Season the pork generously with salt and pepper. Heat the oil in a cast-iron pot or a heavy-based saucepan and brown the pork well, a few pieces at a time. As each batch is browned, transfer to a bowl.

Add the sliced onion and garlic to the pot and stir in the oil for a few minutes to colour. Add the wine and allow to bubble over a high heat for a few minutes, stirring well. Return the browned pork to the pot and cover with a tight-fitting lid. Place in the oven and cook for 60 minutes.

Add the quinces and rosemary to the pot and cook for a further 30 minutes. Remove from the oven and allow to rest for 30 minutes before serving in shallow bowls.

Serves 4

Braised rabbit with mushrooms, chestnuts and shallots

This is a rustic autumn dish to be made when the nights start to lengthen and there's a chill in the evening air. If possible, buy fresh chestnuts at the market and roast and peel them yourself at home; they have a wonderful aroma and flavour. Otherwise, buy frozen ready-peeled chestnuts and roast them in the oven until golden.

2 rabbits, wild if possible
190 ml (6½ fl oz) extra virgin olive oil
salt
freshly ground black pepper
125 g (4 oz) plain (all-purpose) flour
12 golden shallots, peeled, leaving the base intact

250 ml (8½ fl oz) pinot noir
400 g (14 oz) Swiss brown or button mushrooms, quartered (if large)
500 ml (17 fl oz) rabbit or Chicken Stock (page 26)
400 g (14 oz) fresh or frozen chestnuts, peeled and roasted

To prepare the rabbits, first cut the forelegs and the back legs away from the body. Next, use a sharp cook's knife and cut through the backbone at the base of the rib cage and at the top of the hip joints. Make a sharp incision either side of the spine and slice the saddles away from the backbone. You should have 6 pieces from each rabbit: 4 legs and 2 saddles. Reserve the offcuts and carcasses to make stock.

Heat the oil in a heavy-based saucepan or casserole dish. Season the rabbit pieces with salt and pepper and dust lightly with flour. Brown the rabbit pieces well, a few at a time. As each batch is browned, transfer to a bowl.

Add a little more oil to the pan and sauté the shallots until they begin to soften and turn a light golden brown. Add the pinot noir and allow to bubble over a high heat for a few minutes, stirring well. Return the browned rabbit pieces to the pan and add the mushrooms and stock. Cover the pan with a tight-fitting lid and bring to the boil. Lower the temperature as far as possible and simmer for 20 minutes. Add the chestnuts to the pan and cook for another 25 minutes, or until the rabbit is tender and falling from the bones. Taste and adjust the seasonings to your liking.

Serves 6

Chicken casserole with sweet capsicums, tomato and onion

A classic summer casserole that is best made when there is an abundance of ripe tomatoes, onions and capsicums (peppers) in the garden or markets. Use red or yellow capsicums combined with long yellow Hungarian wax peppers and lots of green onions. Green onions are immature onions, eaten when they are first pulled from the ground. The bulbs are a brilliant white and the stems are still fresh and green.

1 x 1.6 kg (3½ lb) free-range chicken
3 red capsicums (peppers)
2 long yellow wax peppers
2 green onions or 10 spring onions (scallions), sliced

2 large ripe tomatoes, sliced
2 cloves garlic, chopped
125 ml (4 fl oz) extra virgin olive oil
salt
freshly ground black pepper

Joint the chicken into thighs, drumsticks and wings and cut each breast in half, keeping it on the bone.

Cut the red capsicums and yellow peppers into halves lengthwise, and remove the stems and seeds. Cut into 4 cm (1½ in) slices.

Arrange the chicken pieces in the bottom of a heavy-based saucepan or casserole dish. Add the capsicums, peppers, onions, tomatoes and garlic and drizzle on the olive oil. Cover the pan with a tight-fitting lid and bring to the boil. Lower the temperature to medium and simmer for 60 minutes. Lower the heat as far as possible and simmer gently for a further 15 minutes. Taste and adjust the seasonings to your liking and serve in shallow bowls.

Serves 4

Braised chicken with green olives, lemon and saffron

We make this chicken dish at A la Grecque and serve it with couscous. It can also be made in the oven in a large baking tray. Just mix all the ingredients together in a bowl, refrigerate and leave them for a couple of hours to marinate the chicken. Cook in a 200°C (400°F) oven for 35 minutes until the chicken is cooked and the skin is crisp and golden.

1 lemon
salt
1 x 1.6 kg (3½ lb) free-range chicken
125 ml (4 fl oz) extra virgin olive oil
2 onions, sliced

2 cloves garlic, sliced
20 threads saffron
200 g (7 oz) green olives, pitted and sliced
500 ml (17 fl oz) Chicken Stock (page 26)
freshly ground black pepper

Use a vegetable peeler to peel fine strips of zest from the lemon. Slice the zest into thin julienne strips. Place them in a small saucepan and cover with boiling water from the kettle. Add a teaspoon of salt and boil for 2–3 minutes. Drain well and reserve the zest.

Joint the chicken into thighs, drumsticks and wings and cut each breast in half, keeping it on the bone.

Heat the oil in a heavy-based saucepan or casserole dish. Season the chicken pieces with salt and pepper and fry the chicken pieces in batches over a high heat until the skin is crisp and golden. As each batch is browned, transfer to a bowl. If the chicken has released a lot of fat, drain some of it away.

Add the onions to the pan and sauté for a few minutes until they begin to soften and turn a light golden brown. Add the garlic, saffron and olives and stir. Return the browned chicken pieces to the pan and add the reserved lemon zest and chicken stock.

Cover the pan with a tight-fitting lid and bring to the boil. Lower the temperature and simmer for 15–20 minutes, or until the chicken is cooked. Taste and adjust the seasoning if necessary. Serve with couscous or Saffron Pilaf (page 169).

Serves 4

Slow-cooked beef with braised eggplant

Cook this dish long and slowly to create a thick, dark sauce. I like to sprinkle the beef liberally with freshly ground black pepper before cooking, which contributes to the good flavour. Make sure that you brown the meat well to begin with and only fry a few pieces at a time so that the meat gets a good colour and doesn't stew instead of fry. I find a cast-iron pot is perfect for this dish as you can keep the temperature high.

1 kg (2 lb 3 oz) stewing steak, cut into 5 cm (2 in) cubes
salt
freshly ground black pepper
125 ml (4 fl oz) extra virgin olive oil

1 onion, sliced
2 cloves garlic, sliced
250 ml (8 ½ fl oz) water
3 eggplants (aubergines), cut into 5 cm (2 in) cubes
190 ml (6 ½ fl oz) corn oil

Season the beef generously with salt and pepper. Heat the olive oil in a cast-iron pot or a heavy-based saucepan and brown the beef well, a few pieces at a time. As each batch is browned, transfer to a bowl.

Add the onion and garlic to the pot and stir in the oil for a few minutes to colour. Return the browned beef to the pot and pour in the water. Cover the pot with a tight-fitting lid and bring to the boil. Lower the temperature as far as possible and simmer for 1½ hours.

Sprinkle the eggplant with salt and sit in a colander for 1 hour. Rinse thoroughly and pat dry. Heat the corn oil in a heavy-based frying pan and sauté the eggplant in batches, until browned all over. Drain on kitchen paper. Add the browned eggplant to the pot with the beef for the final 15–20 minutes of cooking. By the end of the cooking, the beef should be very tender, the eggplant melting and the sauce rich and dark. Serve with boiled waxy potatoes.

Serves 4

Stuffed zucchini with avgolemono

This recipe is perfect for those zucchini (courgettes) that have outgrown the baby stage. Cut them in half and use a sharp knife or apple corer to hollow out a cavity and fill with all sorts of tasty stuffings. Allow three zucchini halves per person.

   Make the Avgolemono (page 160) using the liquid that is released from the zucchini as they cook. It is the perfect sauce to serve with these baked zucchini, as it has a lovely lemony tang and is light and frothy. It's a bit like a hollandaise sauce, but without the richness of all the butter.

....

6 zucchinis (courgettes), 20–23 cm (8–9 ¼ in) long
120 g (4 oz) medium-grain rice, well rinsed under
   running water
300 g (10 ½ oz) minced (ground) lamb
1 small onion, grated
1 clove garlic, finely chopped
1 tablespoon ouzo
½ cup chopped parsley

½ teaspoon ground cumin
½ teaspoon dried oregano
½ teaspoon salt
½ teaspoon ground black pepper
160 ml (5 ½ fl oz) extra virgin olive oil
180 ml (6 fl oz) water
Avgolemono (page 160) to serve

Trim the stalk end from the zucchinis and cut them in half. Use a small sharp vegetable knife or an apple corer to scoop out a cavity from one end of the zucchini to the other, without piercing the skin.

Place the rice in a large mixing bowl with the lamb, onion, garlic, ouzo, parsley, spices, salt and pepper. Add 2 tablespoons of the oil and use your hands to mix everything together thoroughly. Using your fingers, fill the hollows fairly neatly with the stuffing. Arrange the stuffed zucchinis in the base of a large heavy-based saucepan or casserole dish. Pour on the water and remaining olive oil and cover the saucepan with a tight-fitting lid. Bring to the boil, then lower the heat and simmer gently for 30 minutes. Remove from the heat and leave to rest for 15 minutes.

Lift the zucchinis onto a serving dish and use 250 ml (8 ½ fl oz) of the remaining cooking liquid to make the avgolemono.

Divide the stuffed zucchini halves among 4 shallow soup bowls and spoon over a generous amount of avgolemono as you serve.

Serves 4

Braised veal shanks with carrots, mushrooms and chestnuts

This recipe is inspired by one I discovered in Paula Wolfert's book *The Slow Mediterranean Kitchen*. The carrots and onions cook down to a wonderful sweet purée that really complements the silky texture of the slow braised shanks. The mushrooms and chestnuts balance the dish with their nutty flavour and provide a contrasting texture. To my mind, it is a perfect winter dinner.

Ask your butcher to 'french' the shanks for you, which means to trim them neatly and scrape the flesh and sinews from the exposed bones so that they look tidy.

4 veal shanks, frenched if possible
salt
freshly ground black pepper
125 ml (4 fl oz) extra virgin olive oil
250 g (9 oz) pancetta, cut into batons
3 onions, sliced
2 bay leaves
3 sprigs thyme
2 star anise

5 cloves garlic (3 peeled but left whole and
    2 finely chopped)
4 carrots, diced
500 ml (17 fl oz) dry white wine
500 ml (17 fl oz) Chicken Stock (page 26)
2 tablespoons butter
500 g (1 lb 2 oz) Swiss brown or button
    mushrooms, cleaned and quartered
300 g (10 ½ oz) chestnuts, peeled and roasted

Preheat the oven to 160ºC (320ºF).

Season the shanks with salt and pepper. Heat the oil in a heavy-based frying pan. Fry the shanks, two at a time, over a medium heat until evenly browned. As each batch is browned, transfer to a casserole or baking dish.

Add the pancetta, onions, bay leaves, thyme and star anise to the pan and sauté for about 10 minutes, or until the onions are soft and golden. Add the garlic and carrots and sauté for a further 5 minutes, stirring. Tip all the vegetables into the casserole with the shanks.

Pour the wine into the frying pan and allow to bubble over a high heat for a few minutes, stirring well to scrape up any brown bits from the bottom of the pan. Add the chicken stock and boil vigorously for 5 minutes to reduce. Pour onto the shanks and season with salt and pepper.

Cover with a tight-fitting lid and cook in the oven for 60 minutes, or until the shanks are very tender. Lift the shanks out of the casserole and set aside in a warm place until ready to serve.

Remove and discard the bay leaves, thyme and star anise. Strain through a colander, reserving both the braising liquid and the vegetables. Tip the vegetables into a food processor and whiz to a chunky purée. Set aside and keep warm until ready to serve. Return the braising liquid to the casserole and boil until reduced to a thickish sauce.

Heat the butter in a clean frying pan until it starts to froth. Add the mushrooms and sauté for 2–3 minutes. Add the chestnuts to the pan, and sauté for 2–3 minutes, stirring from time to time, until they are warmed through. Add the mushrooms and chestnuts to the sauce.

To serve, spoon a generous amount of vegetable purée on each plate. Sit a shank on top of the purée and drizzle with sauce. Scatter the mushrooms and chestnuts around the shanks and serve.

Serves 4

Braised veal chops with kritharaki

Kritharaki is small rice-shaped pasta that is used in many Greek casseroles. It is also sold in many supermarkets by the Italian name risoni or rosmarino. Kritharaki is usually cooked in the meat juices so that it absorbs the flavours of the dish. It is generally cooked until it is quite soft, instead of al dente.

    The quality of veal chops can vary depending on the age of the animal. For this dish you don't want baby veal, which will dry out in a casserole, so ask your butcher for chops from an animal that is about 6 months old.

....

8 veal chops
salt
freshly ground black pepper
125 ml (4 fl oz) extra virgin olive oil
2 onions, sliced

2 cloves garlic, chopped
250 ml (8 ½ fl oz) dry white wine
1 litre (34 fl oz) veal stock or Chicken Stock
   (page 26)
1 bay leaf
250 g (9 oz) kritharaki or risoni

Heat the oven to 160°C (320°F). Season the chops with salt and pepper.

Heat the oil in a heavy-based frying pan and brown the chops well, a few at a time. As each batch is browned, transfer to a casserole or baking dish.

Add the onions to the frying pan and sauté for a few minutes until they begin to soften and turn a light golden brown. Add the garlic and stir for a minute, then tip into the baking dish with the chops.

Pour the wine into the frying pan and allow to bubble over a high heat for a few minutes, stirring well to scrape up any brown bits from the bottom of the pan. Pour onto the chops then add the stock and the bay leaf.

Cover with a tight-fitting lid and cook in the oven for 45 minutes. Lift the chops out of the casserole and set aside in a bowl.

Add the kritharaki to the casserole and stir in well with ¾ teaspoon of salt. Increase the oven temperature to 180°C (350°F). Return the casserole to the oven, uncovered, for a further 25 minutes, or until the liquid has been absorbed. Return the chops to the casserole dish and leave on the stovetop for 10 minutes to warm through. Serve with a crisp green salad.

Serves 4

Fricassée of lamb and spring vegetables

This dish brings back memories of a holiday in the Southern Peloponnese region of Greece with our children. We had stopped for the night at a village called Aréopolis, and after an evening walk on a lovely rocky beach we wandered back to the village to eat. We were tempted into a small, unassuming restaurant by delicious cooking smells. Three generations of women from one family ran the dining room and there was only one dish on the menu: fricassée of spring lamb offal (variety meats) with greens. It was brilliant and unforgettable.

For those who are daunted by the prospect of eating offal, I have modified the dish using a boned leg of lamb. But if you are tempted by the thought of the original, make the casserole with 1 lamb's liver, 3 kidneys, 2 hearts and 6 sweetbreads.

....

1 kg (2 lb 3 oz) leg of lamb (boned weight)
salt
freshly ground black pepper
190 ml (6 ½ fl oz) extra virgin olive oil

12 spring onions (scallions), roughly chopped
3 stalks green garlic, washed and roughly chopped
1 cos (romaine) lettuce, roughly chopped
½ cup dill, roughly chopped

Trim away the excess fat from the lamb and cut into 3 cm (1 ¼ in) dice. Season with salt and pepper.

Heat the oil in a heavy-based saucepan and sear the lamb quickly, a few pieces at a time, just to brown it. As each batch is browned, transfer to a bowl.

Returned the browned lamb to the pan and add the spring onions, green garlic, lettuce and dill. Stir briefly then cover with a tight-fitting lid. Don't be tempted to add any liquid as the juices released from the meat and vegetables will create a lovely sauce. Lower the heat as far as possible and simmer very gently for 60 minutes. (If using offal, simmer for 30 minutes.) Serve in shallow bowls.

Serves 4

Roast lamb rump with spinach purée, feta and nutmeg

Lamb rumps are ideal for a couple or a small family, as they are sold individually, and are roughly the right size for one serve. So if you're only cooking for two people you're not left with half a leg of lamb to be eaten cold the next day.

Rumps are generally rather lean and they need no trimming or lengthy preparation. Just a quick drizzle of oil, some garlic, herbs, salt and pepper – and they are ready to roast. But if you have time to sit them in a marinade for an hour or so, it adds lots of flavour as well.

....

4 lamb rumps
salt
freshly ground black pepper

Marinade
125 ml (4 fl oz) extra virgin olive oil
1 clove garlic, finely sliced
½ teaspoon ground cumin, lightly roasted
freshly ground black pepper

Spinach purée
500 g (1 lb 2 oz) spinach leaves
2 tablespoons extra virgin olive oil
1 teaspoon freshly ground nutmeg
salt
freshly ground black pepper
150 g (5½ oz) feta cheese

Combine the marinade ingredients in a mixing bowl. Rub over the lamb rumps and leave to marinate for 60 minutes. Remove from the marinade and season lightly with salt and pepper.

Preheat the oven to 220°C (430°F). Heat a heavy ovenproof frying pan over a high heat. Sear the lamb rumps quickly in the dry pan until evenly browned. Transfer the pan to the oven and roast the lamb for 15 minutes. Remove from the oven and rest for 10 minutes before serving.

While the lamb is resting, wash the spinach leaves thoroughly. Place them in a heavy-based saucepan with the residual water and wilt over a high heat. Tip into a colander and drain away any excess liquid. Tip into a food processor and whiz to a purée. Add the oil, nutmeg, salt and pepper and whiz briefly to combine. Transfer to a serving bowl and crumble in the feta. Stir briefly.

To serve, spoon a generous amount of spinach purée onto each plate. Slice the lamb rumps thickly and arrange on top of the spinach. Drizzle with pan juices and serve straight away.

Serves 4

Roast kid with potatoes fourno

This dish requires little preparation and yields succulent results from long, slow roasting. You can also bake the baby goat in a terracotta pot or a deep cast-iron pot with a lid.

Ask your butcher to chop through the leg bone in three places, leaving the meat attached on the underside.

1 x 1.4 kg (3 lb 1 oz) leg of kid
salt
freshly ground black pepper
6 cloves garlic, sliced

8 waxy potatoes, peeled and cut into thick wedges
extra virgin olive oil
500 ml (17 fl oz) water

Preheat the oven to 200°C (400°F). Trim off any excess fat from the meat and rub all over with salt and pepper. Tuck the garlic slices into the 3 deep incisions in the top side of the meat.

Place the leg in a baking tray and arrange the potatoes all around. Season the potatoes with salt and pepper and drizzle everything with olive oil. Bake for 30 minutes, then reduce the temperature to 90–100°C (195–210°F). Pour the water into the baking tray and bake for a further 1½ hours. Serve with a salad of peppery rocket (arugula) or mustard cress.

Serves 4

Roast chicken with anchovy mayonnaise

When the kids where growing up we always had Saturday lunch together. One of our favourite meals was a clear chicken consommé, a crusty baguette and a plate of roast chicken served in the centre of the table for everyone to pick at – either by adding it to the soup or making it into a sandwich. Serve with plenty of the anchovy mayonnaise.

2 onions, roughly chopped
2 carrots, roughly chopped
1 stalk celery, roughly chopped
1 leek, roughly chopped
6 stalks parsley
10 whole black peppercorns
2 litres (68 fl oz) water
1 x 1.7 kg (3 lb 12 oz) free-range chicken
extra virgin olive oil
salt
freshly ground black pepper

Anchovy Mayonnaise
4 egg yolks
1 tablespoon white wine vinegar
250 ml (8 ½ fl oz) corn oil
125 ml (4 fl oz) lemon juice
8 anchovy fillets
dash of tabasco
pinch ground black pepper

Put all the vegetables into a large saucepan with the parsley and peppercorns. Cover with the water. Bring to the boil then lower the heat and simmer gently for 45 minutes.

Rinse the chicken well and pat dry with kitchen paper. Lower it into the vegetable stock and return to a gentle boil. Simmer for 25 minutes, uncovered, skimming away any impurities that rise to the surface.

Preheat the oven to 180°C (350°F). Lift the chicken out of the stock and onto a baking tray. Drizzle with olive oil and sprinkle with salt and pepper. Bake for 40 minutes until the skin is crisp and golden.

Strain the stock through a colander. Taste, and adjust the seasonings to your liking. Keep in the fridge or freezer for handy use, or make into a soup to serve with the roast chicken by adding a cup of frozen green peas and some rice. Simmer gently until the rice is cooked.

To make the mayonnaise, whiz the egg yolks and vinegar in a food processor. Gradually add the oil until the mixture thickens. Add lemon juice until the mayonnaise reaches the desired consistency then add anchovies, tabasco and a pinch of pepper.

Serves 4

Pot-roasted home-grown rooster with leeks and fennel

Chooks (chickens) are a big part of our life at Lorne and breeding them is one of my hobbies. This recipe is for those who share my interest and my all-too frequent despair at the over-supply of roosters in the coop.

Choose a nice plump rooster, and once you've killed, dressed and plucked it, keep it in the fridge for a few days before cooking to tenderise. Singe away any little feathers that are left on the carcass after plucking with cotton balls soaked in a little methylated spirits that you ignite very carefully. Wash the bird thoroughly inside and out and pat dry with paper towel. Cook in a very low oven or on the stove-top.

....

1 x 1.7 kg (3 lb 12 oz) free-range rooster
  (6–7 months old)
salt
freshly ground black pepper
125 ml (4 fl oz) extra virgin olive oil

1 onion, finely sliced
2 leeks, washed and cut into 10 cm (4 in) lengths
1 bulb fennel, sliced
125 ml (4 fl oz) verjuice

Preheat the oven to 150°C (300°F). Season the rooster with salt and pepper, rubbing it into the skin well. Now season the inside cavity.

Heat the oil in a deep cast-iron pot or heavy-based casserole. Brown the rooster on its back first, then turn to brown the breast and legs. Transfer to a plate and set aside.

Add the onions to the pot and sauté for a few minutes until they start to colour. Add the leek and fennel and cook for a few minutes, stirring. Add the verjuice then return the rooster to the pot.

Cover with a tight-fitting lid and roast in the oven for 1½–2 hours. By the end of the cooking, the vegetables should be meltingly soft and the liquid thick and tasty. Remove from the oven and leave to rest for 20 minutes before serving.

Serves 4

Pot-roast of yearling beef

Yearling beef is often dismissed as being a little dull. It has neither the delicacy of baby veal, nor the developed flavour of aged beef, but if you season it generously, brown it well and cook it as a tasty pot-roast, it becomes melting and tasty, in a rich, dark sauce. Serve with any number of salads or vegetable accompaniments. I particularly like boiled waxy potatoes and a tomato and red (Spanish) onion salad.

1 kg (2 lb 3 oz) beef topside (round)
salt
freshly ground black pepper

125 ml (4 fl oz) extra virgin olive oil
250 ml (8 ½ fl oz) water

Trim any sinews from the beef. Season it generously with salt and pepper. Heat the oil in a cast-iron pot or a heavy-based saucepan. When it is sizzling, add the beef to the pot and brown it well over a high heat, turning to colour evenly.

Add the water to the pot and cover with a tight-fitting lid. Lower the temperature as far as possible and simmer for 2 hours. Remove from the heat and leave to rest for 10 minutes before carving into thick slices. Spoon the sauce from the pot over the beef and serve with boiled potatoes or rice pilaf.

Serves 4

Chicken breasts roasted 'en papillote' with Middle Eastern flavours

This is a wonderful dinner party dish as you can marinate the chicken the day before and do all the other cooking preparation well before your guests arrive. It's the ideal no-fuss meal, so you can relax with your friends. Serve with couscous or rice pilaf and a radicchio (Italian chicory) salad dressed with extra virgin olive oil, lemon juice and plenty of salt and pepper. The bitter leaves provide a lovely crunchy contrast to the spices and refresh the palate.

6 x 250 g (9 oz) free-range chicken breasts on the bone, skin left on
a handful of coriander (cilantro) leaves to serve

Marinade
1½ tablespoons Pernod
juice and grated zest of 1 lime
1 tablespoon honey
½ cup pistachio nuts, shelled and chopped

3 teaspoons Dijon mustard
1 tablespoon grated fresh ginger
1 teaspoon ground cinnamon
1 teaspoon ground cumin
½ teaspoon cayenne pepper
2 cloves garlic, finely chopped
6 stalks fresh coriander (cilantro), chopped
125 ml (4 fl oz) extra virgin olive oil
salt

Mix all the marinade ingredients together. Place the chicken breasts in a deep dish and pour on the marinade. Cover and refrigerate overnight.

When ready to cook, preheat the oven to 200°C (400°F).

Remove the chicken from the marinade and season lightly with salt. Cut 6 large squares of baking paper and place a chicken breast in the middle of each. Spoon on a generous amount of the marinade, then gather the edges of the paper together and tie with kitchen string to create parcels. Place the parcels on a baking tray and bake for 35–40 minutes. Break into one of the parcels and check that the chicken is cooked by piercing at the thickest part. The meat should be tender and the juices should run clear.

Unwrap the parcels, reserving the cooking juices, and serve the chicken breasts on a bed of couscous or pilaf. Spoon on the cooking juices, and if you like a touch of heat, add a dollop of harissa. Scatter with coriander leaves and serve with radicchio salad.

Serves 6

Chargrilled lamb souvlaki with bligouri

One of the most popular dishes we ever had on the menu at Kostas Restaurant was lamb souvlaki. It is easy to prepare at home and great for a barbecue. Cut the lamb back straps into 5 cm (2 in) cubes, which is the perfect size for souvlaki. Cook the souvlaki on a chargrill or barbecue on a very high heat, and do resist the temptation to fiddle with them too much. Just turn them over once or twice so they develop a crisp brown exterior, and cook them medium–rare so the lamb is pink and juicy inside.

4 lamb back straps
salt
freshly ground black pepper
Bligouri (page 168) to serve
Tzatzkiki (page 47) to serve

Marinade
1 onion, grated
3 cloves garlic, finely chopped
2 ripe tomatoes, grated, skins discarded
½ teaspoon ground cumin
¼ teaspoon cayenne pepper
125 ml extra virgin olive oil

Trim the back straps to remove any sinew and cut into approximate 5 cm (2 in) cubes (they will be smaller at the tapered end of the back straps).

Mix all the marinade ingredients together. Place the lamb cubes in a deep dish and pour on the marinade. Cover and refrigerate for 4 hours.

Preheat a barbecue or chargrill to high and thread 4–5 pieces of lamb onto 4 metal or bamboo skewers (if using bamboo skewers, soak them in water for 10 minutes to prevent them from burning on the barbecue).

Cook for about 15 minutes, turning once or twice so the surface of the meat becomes crisp and brown all over. Move the souvlaki to the side of the barbecue away from the heat and leave to rest for 5 minutes.

Return the souvlaki to the heat briefly, just to warm through, and serve with a generous spoonful of bligouri and tzatziki.

Serves 4

Pork souvlaki with apples, pancetta and sage

Pork shoulder is particularly well suited to chargrilling as it has some fat marbled through the meat, which keeps it juicy while cooking. I also like to marinate meat for chargrilling or barbecuing, as it adds lots of extra flavour, as well as helping to keep the meat moist as it cooks over the high heat.

These souvlaki go particularly well with the sautéed apples, pancetta and sage.

....

1 kg (2 lb 3 oz) shoulder

Marinade
1 onion
3 cloves garlic
125 ml (4 fl oz) extra virgin olive oil
2 ripe tomatoes
freshly ground black pepper
1 teaspoon chilli flakes

Apples, pancetta and sage
2 tablespoons butter
2 Granny Smith apples, peeled, cored and sliced
1 tablespoon raw sugar
150 g (5½ oz) pancetta, cut into thin strips
3 sprigs sage

Trim some of the fat from the pork, leaving enough to keep it moist on the barbecue. Cut into 5 cm (2 in) cubes.

Put all the marinade ingredients into the bowl of a food processor and whiz to a pulp. Place the pork cubes in a deep dish and pour on the marinade. Cover and refrigerate for 4 hours.

Preheat a barbecue or chargrill to high and thread 4–5 pieces of pork onto 4 metal or bamboo skewers (if using bamboo skewers, soak them in water for 10 minutes to prevent them from burning on the barbecue).

Cook for about 15 minutes, turning once or twice so the surface of the meat becomes crisp and brown all over. Move the souvlaki to the side of the barbecue away from the heat and leave to rest while you cook the apples.

Heat the butter in a frying pan until it froths and starts to colour. Add the apple slices and toss in the butter. Sauté for about 10 minutes until golden, then sprinkle on the sugar. Stir in the pancetta strips and sauté for 5 minutes. Remove the pan from the heat and add the chopped sage. Toss to combine.

Return the souvlaki to the heat briefly, just to warm through, and serve with a generous spoonful of the hot apples.

Serves 4

....

Lamb keftethes

Keftethes are one of the most popular summer dishes in Greece and right through the Middle East, where they are known as köfte. In Greece keftethes are usually made from minced (ground) beef, as lamb is often expensive. At A la Grecque we always use lamb, which is readily available, and because I think it has a sweeter flavour and makes for a tastier dish. The mince should not be too lean. So much the better if there is a little fat in the mix; it will keep the keftethes moist on the barbecue.

Serve with Saffron Pilaf (page 169) or Tomato, Basil and Black Olive Salad (page 84).

....

1 kg (2 lb 3 oz) minced (ground) lamb
2 onions, grated
3 cloves garlic, finely chopped
2 eggs
1 cup chopped parsley
½ cup chopped mint
1 teaspoon ground cumin

1 teaspoon dried oregano
½ teaspoon fresh chilli, finely chopped
1 teaspoon salt
½ teaspoon ground black pepper
1 cup breadcrumbs
1 tablespoon ouzo
125 ml (4 fl oz) extra virgin olive oil

Combine all the ingredients in a large mixing bowl and use your hands to knead everything together well. Leave the mixture for 30 minutes at room temperature to allow the flavours to develop.

Preheat a barbecue or chargrill to high. With wet hands, form the mixture into 16 oval-shaped portions. Cook for about 15 minutes, turning once or twice so the surface of the keftethes become crisp and brown.

Serves 4

....

The little extras

At A la Grecque we try to keep the menu as simple as possible. We trade on our reputation for having the best quality seafood and only buy produce in small quantities so that things are fresh every day. Preparing and presenting the dishes in a minimalist style, with an accompanying sauce and a selection of side dishes for diners to choose from, mirrors the way we eat at home.

Sauces and accompaniments

As often as possible I like to prepare dinner around whatever is growing in the garden that I can pick freshly. So I might serve up a small piece of tuna, grilled (broiled) rare with a dollop of piperade and a roasted baby beetroot (beet) salad; or perhaps a few local whiting with rocket leaves and agresto sauce made from basil, parsley and garlic — all of it picked straight from the garden.

Leftovers from a roast lamb or chicken are considerably more interesting when served with ravigote sauce — a full-flavoured combination of herbs, mustard and salty capers. Green sauce can be made to enhance a meal of octopus or kalamari. Almost any left over sauce can be kept in the fridge for a few days and served on toast with some slices of ripe tomato and feta for a light lunch.

On my early visits to Greece when I was served the classic avgolemono I was reluctant to allow myself to enjoy it. It brought back bad childhood memories of inexpertly made egg flip. But as I learnt how to make it myself, whisking the eggs thoroughly and cooking them properly so they are light and frothy, I realise now what a great addition it is to many dishes, especially zucchini (courgettes) stuffed with lamb and rice. It makes a good dish great.

I love to eat fish with rice. The combination seems to me so wholesome and complete. And by adding saffron to the pilaf, and drizzling a little Sauce à la Grecque onto the fish, you might think you've gone to heaven…

Egg and lemon sauce
Avgolemono

This is a versatile sauce that can be served with many white meat dishes, such as chicken or veal. It is generally not served with red meat as it is made using a white stock or the cooking liquid from the dish with which it is to be served. In Greece it is also served with special soups that are made from the offal (variety meats) of the Easter lamb, which is spit-roasted over charcoals on Easter Sunday in every front garden in the village.

Avgolemono has a similar frothy texture to hollandaise sauce but without the butter.

....

250 ml (8 ½ fl oz) Chicken Stock (page 26),
    or the cooking juices from any other
    meat you are preparing
3 egg yolks
juice of 2 lemons
1 teaspoon chopped dill (optional)

In a small saucepan, bring the stock to a boil.

Whisk the egg yolks, lemon juice together in a stainless steel bowl then slowly drizzle in the boiling stock. Whisk vigorously until the sauce is thick and frothy. You might want to sit the bowl over a pan of simmering water and whisk continuously until it thickens. Fold in the chopped dill and serve while warm.

Serves 6

Latholemono

This is another traditional Greek sauce that is ideal for serving with chargrilled fish and seafood.

....

125 ml (4 fl oz) extra virgin olive oil
60 ml (2 fl oz) lemon juice
salt
freshly ground black pepper
1 teaspoon finely chopped parsley or
    dill (optional)

Combine all the ingredients in a mixing bowl and whisk until well combined. If not using straight away, store the latholemono in the fridge for up to 2 days. Whisk before using to recombine.

Serves 6

Aïoli

250 ml (8 ½ fl oz) vegetable oil
5 cloves garlic, peeled but left whole
3 egg yolks
60 ml (2 fl oz) white wine vinegar
60 ml (2 fl oz) lemon juice
salt
freshly ground black pepper
dash of Tabasco

Place the oil and garlic cloves in a saucepan and slowly bring to the boil. Lower the heat and simmer gently for 30 minutes. Remove from the heat and leave to cool completely before using.

Place the egg yolks and vinegar in the bowl of a food processor. Whiz to combine. With the motor running, slowly drizzle in the garlic oil together with the garlic cloves, until the mixture emulsifies to form a mayonnaise. If it looks very oily and thick, add enough lemon juice to thin to the desired consistency. Season to taste with salt and pepper and a dash of Tabasco.

Serves 6

Agresto

This sauce is similar to pesto and can be used in the same way. Serve with pasta, as a dip with crudités, or as an accompaniment to grilled (broiled) fish. I think it makes the perfect lunch when spread on bruschetta and topped with rocket (arugula) and parmesan. Depending on how you plan to serve the agresto, you can make it smooth or chunky, runny or thick, by adding more or less oil or verjuice.

125 g (4 oz) blanched almonds
125 g (4 oz) walnuts
1 clove garlic, roughly chopped
1 cup flat-leaf (Italian) parsley
6 basil leaves
½ teaspoon salt
¼ teaspoon freshly ground black pepper
90 ml (3 fl oz) extra virgin olive oil
90 ml (3 fl oz) verjuice

Preheat the oven to 180°C (350°F). Scatter the almonds and walnuts onto separate baking trays and roast for 10 minutes. Tip the walnuts into a tea (dish) towel and rub vigorously to remove as much of the skin as you can. Set almonds and walnuts aside to cool.

Place the almonds and walnuts in the bowl of a food processor. Add the garlic, herbs, salt and pepper and whiz until fairly smooth. With the motor running, drizzle in the oil, followed by the verjuice, to make a thickish paste. Taste and adjust the seasonings to your liking.

Use straight away or store in an airtight jar, covered with a thin film of olive oil. The agresto will keep for a week in the fridge.

Serves 6

Sauce à la grecque

This sauce was the inspiration for the name of our restaurant and for many years we have served it as an accompaniment to grilled (broiled) fish dishes. The recipe is from Greg and Lucy Malouf's book, *Arabesque*. The saffron and spices, the honey and touch of chilli all combine to make a perfectly balanced dressing.

....

10 threads saffron
1 teaspoon honey
60 ml (2 fl oz) red wine vinegar
60 ml (2 fl oz) white wine
10 shallots, finely chopped
3 cloves garlic, sliced
1 bullet chilli
1 teaspoon fennel seeds
1 teaspoon coriander seeds
½ teaspoon white peppercorns
250 ml (8½ fl oz) extra virgin olive oil
125 ml (4 fl oz) lemon juice
salt
freshly ground black pepper

Combine the saffron, honey, vinegar and wine in a saucepan and heat gently, stirring to dissolve the honey. Add the shallots, garlic and chilli and simmer very gently for 10 minutes. Remove from the heat and leave to cool.

Scatter the fennel and coriander seeds and the peppercorns in a frying pan and toast over a low heat for a few minutes until fragrant. Leave to cool slightly then grind in a mortar and pestle or spice grinder.

Combine the cooled vinegar mixture and ground spices of a food processor and whiz to mix. With the motor running, drizzle in the olive oil, then the lemon juice. Taste and season with salt and pepper to your liking. If not using straight away, store the sauce in the fridge for up to 2 days.

Serves 12

Parsley and tahini sauce

The combination of yoghurt, tahini and lemon juice gives this sauce an exotic Middle Eastern flavour. It goes especially well with roast chicken or Lamb Keftethes (page 154).

....

2 cups flat-leaf (Italian) parsley leaves
3 spring onions (scallions)
1 clove garlic
1 slice stale sourdough bread, roughly chopped
1 tablespoon pine nuts, lightly roasted
60 ml (2 fl oz) plain yoghurt
60 ml (2 fl oz) tahini
80 ml (2½ fl oz) extra virgin olive oil
juice of ½ lemon
salt
freshly ground black pepper

Combine the parsley, spring onions, garlic, bread, pine nuts, yoghurt and tahini in the bowl of a food processor and whiz to form a fairly smooth sauce. Add the oil and lemon juice then season with salt and pepper.

Use straight away or store in an airtight jar in the fridge for up to 3 days.

Serves 6

Romesco

Romesco is a Spanish sauce that is great to serve with meat or fish. It combines toasted nuts and bread with the sweet-sourness of tomatoes, capsicums (peppers) and vinegar and the heat of chilli. These elements should be well balanced with no single flavour dominating.

3 large ripe tomatoes, halved
175 ml (6 fl oz) extra virgin olive oil
salt
freshly ground black pepper
150 g (5½ oz) whole blanched almonds
60 ml (2 fl oz) red wine vinegar

60 ml (2 fl oz) white wine
6 cloves garlic
2 bullet chillies
1 red capsicum (pepper), cut into 2 cm (¾ in)
    strips
3 thick slices stale sourdough

Preheat the oven to 200°C (400°F) and lightly oil a baking tray.

Arrange the tomatoes in the baking tray, cut side up. Drizzle with 1 tablespoon of the olive oil, sprinkle with salt and pepper and roast for 20 minutes, or until they are soft and slightly caramelised.

Scatter the almonds on another baking tray and roast for 10 minutes, or until golden brown.

Combine the vinegar, white wine, garlic, chilli and strips of red capsicum in a saucepan and bring to the boil. Simmer for 5 minutes until the capsicum is soft. Tip into a colander and drain.

Heat 2 tablespoons of the oil in a frying pan and fry the bread slices until crisp and golden. Drain briefly on kitchen paper then transfer the bread to the bowl of a food processor. Add the almonds and whiz until coarsely ground. Add the drained capsicum, garlic and chilli with the roasted tomatoes and the rest of the oil. Process to form a chunky sauce. Taste and adjust the seasoning to your liking.

Use straight away or store in an airtight jar in the fridge for up to 3 days.

Serves 8

Anchovy butter

This tangy butter is fantastic spread on thin slices of sourdough toast to serve with a radish salad as part of a table of shared mezze dishes. Alternatively, you can shape it into a fat log and roll up in plastic wrap to store in the fridge or freezer. Cut off slices as needed, and serve on chargrilled steak or a plate of steamed asparagus.

150 g (5 oz) softened butter
8 anchovies
⅓ cup chopped parsley leaves
freshly ground black pepper

Whiz the butter in a food processor until soft. Add the remaining ingredients and whiz again to combine. Scrape into a ramekin and refrigerate. Alternatively, spoon onto a sheet of plastic wrap and roll into a fat log. Twist the ends securely and chill until required. The butter will keep in the fridge for 2 weeks or up to 3 months in the freezer.

Serves 8

Salsa fresca

This is a lovely summery salsa to serve with any grilled (broiled) fish. Use full-flavoured ripe tomatoes, for sweetness and don't mix the salad too much or it will go mushy. You only need to toss the ingredients gently so they are just combined.

....

4 ripe tomatoes, cut into 1 cm (½ in) dice
1 avocado, cut into 1 cm (½ in) dice
½ telegraph (long) cucumber, cut into
   1 cm (½ in) dice
1 red (Spanish) onion, cut into 1 cm (½ in) dice
1 cup coriander (cilantro) leaves
1 bullet chilli, finely chopped and seeds removed
salt
freshly ground black pepper
125 ml (4 fl oz) extra virgin olive oil
juice of 1 lemon

Combine the vegetables, coriander leaves and chilli in a serving bowl. Season with salt and pepper then drizzle on the olive oil and lemon juice. Toss gently to combine and serve straight away.

Serves 8

Green sauce

A great all-purpose sauce that can be made with endless variations. Try substituting any green herb, such as dill, mint or chervil. Don't be tempted to add lemon juice or the sauce will lose its lovely vibrant green colour. The capers, olives and gherkins (dill pickles) will add enough acidity to balance the olive oil. Serve with all kinds of seafood, but especially kalamari and chargrilled cuttlefish.

....

2 cups flat-leaf (Italian) parsley
½ cup fresh oregano leaves
3 tablespoons capers
2 gherkins (dill pickles)
1 clove garlic
½ cup pitted green olives
2 anchovies
120 ml (4 fl oz) extra virgin olive oil
freshly ground black pepper to taste

Place all the ingredients in the bowl of a food processor and whiz to combine.

Use straight away or store in an airtight jar in the fridge for up to 3 days.

Serves 6

Ravigote

This sauce is full of bold flavours and is ideal to serve with pickled meats, tongue, ham, prosciutto or cold roast lamb. You can substitute parsley for the chervil if you can't find it at the greengrocer, but chervil is very easy to grow and deserves a place in your vegetable garden for its delicate flavour.

....

½ bunch chervil, leaves picked and
    finely chopped
½ bunch French tarragon, leaves picked and
    finely chopped
1 small red (Spanish) onion, finely diced
6 gherkins (dill pickles) or cornichons, finely
    diced
1 tablespoon capers, rinsed and dried
2 teaspoons seeded mustard
190 ml (6½ fl oz) extra virgin olive oil
125 ml (4 fl oz) lemon juice
salt
freshly ground black pepper

Combine all the ingredients in a large mixing bowl. Taste and adjust the seasonings to your liking. Use straight away or store in an airtight jar in the fridge, where it will keep for up to 1 week.

Serves 8

Piperade

This brightly coloured ragoût of capsicums (peppers) makes a perfect accompaniment to any fish dish. The sweetness of the capsicums and tomatoes is especially good with the slight oiliness of chargrilled tuna or salmon.

....

3 red capsicums (peppers), halved lengthwise
3 yellow capsicums (peppers), halved lengthwise
125 ml (4 fl oz) extra virgin olive oil
2 onions, sliced
2 cloves garlic, finely chopped
2 ripe tomatoes, halved and coarsely grated,
    skins discarded
½ cup sliced black olives

Remove the stalks and seeds from the capsicums and slice them lengthwise into 2 cm (¾ in) strips.

Heat the oil in a deep saucepan and fry the capsicums until they start to soften and colour. Stir in the onion and garlic and fry gently for 10 minutes, stirring to prevent them from sticking. Stir in the tomato pulp and simmer for 15 minutes. Add the olives and simmer for a further 5 minutes. Remove from the heat and serve at room temperature.

Serves 8

Prassoriso

This is a similar dish to Spanakoriso (page 170), but made using leeks instead of spinach. It can be eaten as a meal on its own or as a perfect accompaniment to pork dishes. The spinach is optional, but it adds a bit of colour.

....

4 leeks, sliced lengthwise and well washed
3 cloves garlic, finely chopped
125 ml (4 fl oz) extra virgin olive oil
100 g (3½ oz) rice, preferably risotto or arborio, rinsed until the water runs clear
1 teaspoon salt
½ teaspoon freshly ground black pepper
a handful of washed spinach leaves (optional), to serve

Slice the washed leeks finely and place in a heavy-based saucepan. Stir in the garlic, pour on the olive oil and cover the pan with a lid. Cook over a moderate heat for a few minutes, or until the leeks just begin to wilt. Tip the rice onto the leeks and season with salt and pepper. Cover the pan and cook over a very low heat for about 15–20 minutes, or until the rice is cooked. Stir occasionally to prevent the rice from sticking to the bottom and burning.

When the rice is cooked, remove the pan from the heat. Add the spinach leaves, if using, and stir briefly over the heat until they wilt.

Serves 4

Bligouri

Bligouri (coarse cracked wheat) has a lovely nutty flavour and an interesting texture and I often serve it with meat dishes as a change from rice. Alternatively, I'll cook it with chicken stock, add some fresh tarragon and serve it with a roast chicken dinner.

....

2 tablespoons extra virgin olive oil
½ onion, diced
1 clove garlic, finely chopped
200 g (7 oz) bligouri
½ teaspoon salt
500 ml (17 fl oz) boiling water

Heat the oil in a heavy-based saucepan. Add the onion and garlic and sauté until golden. Add the bligouri and stir in the salt. Pour on the boiling water and stir briefly. Lower the heat to a gentle simmer then cover the saucepan and cook for about 15 minutes until all the liquid has been absorbed.

Serves 8

Variations

(i) Stir in ½ cup chopped roasted walnuts and ½ cup parsley leaves to the cooked bligouri.

(ii) Cook the bligouri with 250 ml (8½ fl oz) boiling water. When absorbed, add 250 ml (8½ fl oz) tomato purée and cook for 5 minutes. Stir in ½ teaspoon finely chopped chilli and ½ cup chopped coriander (cilantro) leaves before serving.

Saffron pilaf

Some people tell me that they don't like the taste of saffron. Maybe it's an acquired taste, but I think that it takes a pilaf to another level. Adjust the amount of saffron to suit your taste, but make sure that it doesn't dominate. Serve with any fish or chicken dish..

440 ml (15 fl oz) Chicken Stock (page 26)
2 tablespoons extra virgin olive oil
½ small onion, diced
½ clove garlic, finely chopped
10 strands saffron

220 g (8 oz) golden rice, well rinsed under
    cold running water
½ teaspoon salt
freshly ground black pepper

Heat the stock in a saucepan until it reaches boiling point.

Heat the oil in a heavy-based saucepan. Add the onion and garlic and sauté gently for about 5 minutes, until soft and translucent. Add the saffron, followed by the rice. Season with salt and a pinch of pepper and stir together well. Pour on the boiling stock and stir gently. Lower the heat to a gentle simmer, cover the saucepan and cook for about 15 minutes until all the liquid has been absorbed. Serve straight away, or remove the pan from the heat and cover the rice with a tea towel until required.

Serves 4

Spinach rice Spanakoriso

Translating literally as 'spinach rice', this is a simple dish to make but it will surprise you with its flavours. In Greece it is often eaten as a meal in its own right, but without the egg it also makes a lovely accompaniment to lamb dishes. The excess water on the washed spinach and the liquid that it releases are sufficient to cook the rice. It absorbs the flavours of the oil and spinach as it cooks. Don't be tempted to add any water unless the rice is really sticking to the bottom of the pan – in which case you probably have the heat too high.

1 kg (2 lb 3 oz) spinach leaves, thoroughly washed
125 ml (4 fl oz) extra virgin olive oil
100 g (3½ oz) rice, preferably risotto or arborio,
   rinsed until the water runs clear

1 teaspoon salt
½ teaspoon freshly ground black pepper
slices of feta cheese to serve
4 poached eggs to serve

Place the spinach in heavy-based saucepan. Pour on the oil and cover the pan with a lid. Cook over a moderate heat for a few minutes, or until the spinach just begins to wilt. Tip the rice onto the spinach without stirring and season with salt and pepper. Cover the pan and cook over a very low heat for 15–20 minutes, or until the rice is cooked. Stir occasionally to prevent the rice from sticking to the bottom and burning.

Serve the spanakoriso topped with a slice of feta and a poached egg.

Serves 4

Fattoush

This is a light and refreshing salad to accompany grilled (broiled) fish, such as King George whiting, John Dory, rock flathead or flounder, which have a more delicate flavour than oilier fish. Add the lavoche at the last minute, just before serving, so that it retains its crunchiness. It will soak up the combination of flavours from the salad vegetables and the dressing on the plate.

3 large ripe tomatoes, cut into 1 cm dice
½ telegraph (long) cucumber, skin on, cut into
    1 cm (½ in) dice
1 red (Spanish) onion, cut into 1 cm (½ in) dice
5 red radishes, cut into 1 cm (½ in) dice
6 sprigs mint, leaves picked and roughly torn
6 sprigs coriander (cilantro), leaves picked and
    roughly torn
6 sprigs flat-leaf (Italian) parsley, leaves picked
    and roughly torn
50 g (1¾ oz) Lavoche (page 182)

Dressing
juice of 1 lime
1 tablespoon pomegranate molasses
125 ml (4 fl oz) extra virgin olive oil
salt
freshly ground black pepper

Combine all the vegetables and herbs in a large mixing bowl and toss together gently. The salad can be prepared to this point up to a couple of hours ahead of time.

Just before serving, break the lavoche into small pieces and scatter onto the salad. Whisk together the dressing ingredients and pour over the salad. Toss gently and serve straight away.

Serves 8–10

Skorthalia

There are as many variations of skorthalia as there are housewives in Greece. Some women like to add ground almonds or breadcrumbs to the mix, but basically it is a very garlicky potato purée, which can be liquid enough to serve as a sauce or thick enough to serve as a vegetable accompaniment. There is even a famous Greek song that goes, 'I will fry you fish with beetroot and skorthalia' — a true declaration of love!

4 large waxy potatoes, peeled and cubed
10 cloves garlic
½ teaspoon salt

190 ml (6 ½ fl oz) extra virgin olive oil
freshly ground black pepper

Place the potatoes and garlic in a large saucepan. Add the salt and enough cold water just to cover. Bring to the boil, then simmer for about 15 until the potatoes are soft and beginning to break up.

Drain, keeping back a little of the cooking water with the potatoes. Mash the potatoes by hand, gradually beating in the oil. Don't be tempted to use a mixer for this or the potatoes will be gluey. Taste and adjust the seasoning to your liking.

Serves 6

Easter

Easter in Greece is the most important celebration of the year, for religious and non-religious people alike. Families come together as city people return to their villages of origin. New clothes are bought for wearing to Midnight Mass, religious rituals are re-enacted, the lamb is slaughtered with great care, a feast is prepared, and on Easter Sunday music, dancing and merriment ring out from every front garden.

The Greek Orthodox religion prescribes forty days of fasting before Easter, in much the same way as other Christian denominations have a Lenten fast from Ash Wednesday. The Greek Orthodox fast requires participants to abstain from eating meat, eggs or dairy products for forty days, and in the Holy Week that precedes Easter Sunday the fast extends to fish and any creatures that have blood (octopus is allowed and so are prawns/shrimp).

The Saturday night sees everyone immaculately groomed for the reunion with old friends and cousins at the church. Elaborately decorated candles are purchased and carried with pride to church where they receive the 'Light of the World'. The lights in the Church are extinguished, and at the stroke of midnight, the priest pronounces 'Christos anesti!' (Christ has risen!). He opens the door of the nave of the church, holding three lighted candles that represent the Father, the Son and the Holy Ghost. All the small children surge forward, eager to be the first to light their candle from the priest's and then to pass on the light to the rest of the congregation. The lighted candles are carefully carried home and a sign of the cross is made on the doorstep of each house to protect the family from evil.

Yiayia and Papou were with us in Australia one year when Greek Easter came around. Yiayia showed me how to dye eggs red (the colour represents fertility and the eggs symbolise new life) and to make a special lentil soup on Good Friday (the little round lentils represent the Virgin Mary's tears). Yiayia made her soup without olive oil, in the strictest form of abstinence. I don't feel the need to be quite so strict, so I always add olive oil and spinach to the soup for extra flavour.

From Yiayia I also learnt how to make the traditional Easter tsoureki. Making and eating tsoureki is definitely my favourite part of the Easter celebrations. It is a rich bread, similar to brioche and it is eaten everywhere to celebrate the end of the fast. Tsoureki is full of eggs and butter and is flavoured with masticha, which gives it a wonderfully exotic aroma. Masticha comes from trees that grow wild on the Greek island of Chios near the west coast of Turkey. Tiny resinous crystals are collected when the trees are 'bled', and these are then ground to form the masticha powder. Another spice called mahlepi (made from the ground kernels of wild cherries) gives the tsoureki a unique nutty flavour.

The tsoureki loaves are plaited, sprinkled with flaked almonds and often curled into a circle with a red egg in the centre. In some areas of Greece, different special breads and pastries are made for Easter – a friend who comes from the island of Limnos always made koulourakia biscuits, flavoured with lemon zest – but they all contain butter and eggs to break the fast.

177

Breads and pastries

Greek families eat bread with every meal. It has always been the cheapest way to bulk out a meal and fill an empty stomach during times of poverty, and although we now live in times of plenty, bread remains an essential part of every Greek table.

In her younger years, Yiayia would make a loaf of bread every Saturday to take to church on Sunday morning. The little round loaf would be impressed with ancient Greek holy words and symbols from her special wooden stamp. It was blessed by the priest, then cut up and given out at the end of the service as a part of the Holy Communion.

Traditionally, most households in the Greek village had an outdoor oven, similar to a wood-fired pizza oven, and bread was made for the family twice a week. The oven would be fuelled with straw and when it had all burnt and the roof of the oven was white hot, it was the correct temperature to bake the bread. As well as standard loaves, all sorts of other pitas and boureks would be made from bits of spare dough and any filling which was to hand (mainly egg and cheese), and the children would gather around waiting for these tasty bits to be shared around. These days most villages have a bakery and the art of keeping the sourdough 'starter' alive and making bread by hand is all but lost.

At A la Grecque we make many different types of breads and pastries. We have a large old pizza oven and the stone base is ideal for cooking piadina, pizza and grissini. I always prefer to make my own filo pastry for spanakotiropita, pastourmopita and sweets such as patzavoura and baklava, as it is far superior to the factory-made filo pastry that is commercially available. However, it is very time consuming to make, so I sometimes buy handmade emek yufka (which is similar to filo) from Greek or Turkish supermarkets as an acceptable alternative.

Working with yeast in dough is a sensual and satisfying experience. Feeling the elasticity of the dough while kneading, watching it rise, knocking it back, proving it, enjoying the aroma as it bakes, and most of all, eating warm, crusty bread or cinnamon rolls, fresh from the oven with lashings of butter – these are all homely, comforting and immensely pleasurable sensations.

Turkish flat breads are simple to make for a party or a barbecue and can have many uses. They can be used to wrap up a souvlaki with some salad, they can be dipped into taramosalata, topped with kephalograviera and grilled (broiled), or just used to mop up the sauce on the plate.

Lavoche is also a versatile addition to any pantry and you can make it with whatever flavourings you want: ground black pepper, poppy seeds, sesame seeds, ras-el-hanout or coarse sea salt are all good. Serve lavoche with cheese, crumble into a fattoush salad, dip it into a bowl of hummus, or best of all, enjoy it with slices of avocado and perfectly ripe tomato.

Village bread Horiatiko psomi

To encourage the development of a good crust, use a plastic spray bottle to spray water into the oven at the start of the baking time and then again towards the end of the cooking time. This creates steam, which helps a firm crust to form.

20 g (¾ oz) fresh yeast
600 ml (20½ fl oz) warm water
1 kg (2 lb 3 oz) baker's flour

10 g (¼ oz) gluten flour
25 g (1 oz) salt
20 g (¾ oz) full-cream powdered milk

Mix the yeast with 3 tablespoons of the warm water to form a creamy paste.

Sift both the flours and the salt onto a work surface and mix in the powdered milk. Make a well in the centre and pour in the yeast with the remaining warm water. Mix together well then knead for 15 minutes to form a smooth, elastic dough. You can do this by hand or with an electric mixer fitted with a dough hook. Shape the dough into a ball and place in an oiled bowl. Cover with plastic wrap and leave in a warm place for about 2 hours until the dough has doubled in size.

Scoop the dough out onto your work surface and knead for a few minutes. Divide it in half and shape into 2 round cobs. Place them on a lightly greased baking tray. Brush each cob with water and dust with flour. With a sharp knife, slash the surface into a diamond shape grid. Leave in a warm place for 30 minutes to rise again.

While the dough is rising for the second time, preheat the oven to 220°C (430°F). Bake the loaves for 35 minutes, spraying with water twice during the baking time. The cooked bread should sound hollow when tapped.

Makes 2 loaves

Turkish flat breads

These flat breads are perfect for any occasion that calls for eating with your hands. Cook them on the barbecue then use them to wrap around a salad or a sausage. They can also be topped with grilled (broiled) soutzouk (Turkish sausage), served with dips or used to make souvlakis.

....

500 g (1 lb 2 oz) plain (all-purpose) flour
3 teaspoons red wine vinegar
3 tablespoons extra virgin olive oil
1 teaspoon salt
250 ml (8 ½ fl oz) cold water

Place all the ingredients in a food processor and whiz until the mixture combines to form a ball. Wrap in plastic wrap and refrigerate for 1 hour.

While the dough is resting, preheat a charcoal grill, barbecue or flat griddle plate to high. Divide the dough into 8 portions and shape into round balls. Roll into flat rounds, about 20 cm x 5 mm (8 in x ¼ in) thick. Stack the rounds on a plate, dusting with semolina and separating with sheets of baking paper to stop them sticking together.

Cook over charcoal or on the barbecue, turning once, until puffed up and golden brown on both sides. Serve hot from the grill.

Makes 8

Basic pizza dough

This pizza dough can also be used to make calzone (stuffed pizza) and breads such as ciabatta, foccacia and Grissini (page 182).

....

2 teaspoons dry yeast
2 teaspoons sugar
250 ml (8 ½ fl oz) warm water
500 g (1 lb 2 oz) plain (all-purpose) flour
1 teaspoon salt
100 ml (3 ½ fl oz) extra virgin olive oil

Dissolve the yeast and sugar in the warm water and leave in a warm place for about 10 minutes until it starts to froth up.

Sift the flour and salt into a large mixing bowl. Pour the frothy yeast into the flour and add 1 tablespoon of the oil. Mix together well then knead for 10 minutes to form a smooth, elastic dough. You can do this by hand or with an electric mixer fitted with a dough hook. Shape the dough into a ball and place in an oiled bowl. Cover with plastic wrap and leave in a warm place for at least 1 hour until the dough has doubled in size.

Preheat the oven to 220°C (430°F).

Scoop the dough out onto your work surface and knead for a few minutes. Divide into 6 x 120 g (4 oz) portions and roll out to 25 cm (10 in) rounds. Lift onto pizza trays and brush lightly with olive oil. Spread with your choice of topping and bake for 8–10 minutes or until crisp and golden brown. Serve hot from the oven.

Makes 6 pizza bases

Grissini

Grissini are an essential addition to an antipasto plate as they are perfect finger food. They can be wrapped with thin slices of prosciutto or served with all kinds of dips.

....

1 quantity Basic Pizza Dough (page 181)
sesame seeds or poppy seeds (optional)

Preheat the oven to 220°C (430°F) and line a baking tray with baking paper.

Roll the dough into a 20 cm x 30 cm x 2 cm (8 in x 12 in x ¾ in) rectangle. Use a sharp knife or pizza cutter to cut the dough into 2 cm (¾ in) strips. Press lightly into your choice of sesame or poppy seeds (if using) or twist each strip along its length. Transfer to the baking tray and bake for 10 minutes, until crisp and golden brown.

Transfer to a wire rack to cool before serving, or store in an airtight container.

Makes about 25

Lavoche

Lavoche are crunchy dry biscuits (crackers) that can be served with cheese or quince paste, with mezze or crumbled into a salad. They will last a week in an airtight container.

....

500 g (1 lb 2 oz) plain (all-purpose) flour
1 teaspoon baking powder
½ teaspoon sea salt flakes
2 tablespoons sesame seeds, poppy seeds or
    coarsely ground black pepper
1 teaspoon sugar
250 ml (8 ½ oz) milk
1 teaspoon extra virgin olive oil

Sift the flour into the bowl of a food processor with the baking powder, salt and seeds or pepper. Dissolve the sugar in the milk. Add to the dry ingredients together with the olive oil. Whiz until the mixture combines to form a ball. Wrap in plastic wrap and refrigerate for 1 hour.

Preheat the oven to 180°C (350°F) and lightly oil a baking tray.

Divide the dough into 6 pieces and roll out into very thin sheets or use a pasta machine, working it through the settings. Lift the sheets onto the tray and cut into triangles with a sharp knife or pizza cutter. Bake for 15 minutes in batches, until crisp and golden. Transfer to a wire rack to cool before serving, or store in an airtight container.

Makes about 50

Piadina

Strictly speaking, piadini is an Italian flat bread, but we serve it at A la Grecque because it cooks perfectly on the stone base of our pizza oven. We use it like pita bread to accompany a bowl of Taramosalata (page 48), Melitzanosalata (page 47) or hummus.

The beef dripping (or duck fat) is important for flavour, but at a pinch you could use butter instead.

....

500 g (1 lb 2 oz) plain (all-purpose) flour
1 teaspoon baking powder
1 teaspoon salt
3 teaspoons beef dripping or duck fat

250 ml (8 ½ oz) cold water
garlic oil (optional)
few sprigs rosemary

Sift the flour into the bowl of a food processor with the baking powder and salt. Add the fat and whiz until it is incorporated. With the motor running, drizzle in the water and whiz until the mixture forms a ball. Wrap in plastic wrap and refrigerate for 1 hour.

While the dough is resting, preheat the oven to 250°C (485°F). Divide the dough into 6–8 portions and shape into round balls. Roll each ball into a flat round, about 20 cm x 5 mm (8 in x ¼ in) thick.

Lift each piadina onto a baking tray, drizzle with garlic oil (if using) and sprinkle with rosemary. Bake for 7 minutes. If you have a stone in your oven, remove the piadinas from the baking tray after 5 minutes and place them directly onto the stone to cook for another 2 minutes, or until crisp and golden. Cut into triangles while hot.

Makes 6–8

Savoury cheese, mint and sultana cake

A Greek Cypriot recipe, given to me by a neighbour, Kyria Niki Landos. It is very simple and quick to put together.

530 g (1 lb 3 oz) self-raising flour
200 g (7 oz) sultanas (golden raisins)
1 cup mint leaves, chopped
300 g (10 ½ oz) grated cheddar cheese

6 eggs
375 ml (12 ½ fl oz) corn oil
125 g (4 fl oz) butter, melted
50 g (2 oz) sesame seeds

Preheat the oven to 180°C (350°F) and grease and line a 23 cm (9 in) cake tin.

Sift the flour into a large mixing bowl. Stir in the sultanas, mint and cheese.

In a separate mixing bowl, beat the eggs with the oil and the melted butter. Pour into the flour mixture and stir to combine. Spoon the mixture into the cake tin and sprinkle the surface with sesame seeds. Bake for 1 hour then remove from the oven and cool on a wire rack. Serve at room temperature.

Serves 12

Cardamom and cinnamon rolls

These fragrant rolls are lovely for breakfast or brunch and are also ideal for school lunches. If you want fresh rolls for breakfast, make the dough the day before, cut it into bun shapes and leave them on a tray in the fridge overnight. The next morning, bring them to room temperature before baking. The delicious aromas will have everyone out of bed and waiting at the breakfast table!

....

5 teaspoons dry yeast
180 g (6 ½ oz) sugar
310 ml (10 ½ fl oz) warm water
155 g (5 ½ oz) unsalted butter, melted
3 eggs, lightly beaten
1 tablespoon powdered milk

800 g (1 lb 12 oz) plain (all-purpose) flour
½ teaspoon salt
125 g (4 oz) sugar
2 tablespoons ground cinnamon
3 tablespoons ground cardamom

Mix the yeast and sugar with the warm water and 90 g (3 oz) of the melted butter and leave in a warm place for about 10 minutes until it starts to froth up. Stir in the eggs and powdered milk until well combined.

Sift the flour and salt into a large mixing bowl. Pour the yeast mixture into the flour and mix well to combine. Knead for 10 minutes to form a smooth, elastic dough. You can do this by hand or with an electric mixer fitted with a dough hook. Shape the dough into a ball and place in an oiled bowl. Cover with plastic wrap and leave in a warm place for about 1 hour until the dough has doubled in size.

Preheat the oven to 180°C (350°F) and lightly grease a baking tray.

Scoop the dough out onto your work surface and knead for a few minutes. Roll into a 30 cm x 40 cm (12 in x 16 in) rectangle. Brush with the remaining melted butter and sprinkle with sugar, cinnamon and cardamom. With the longer side facing you, roll the dough up like a Swiss roll. Cut into 5 cm (2 in) slices. Lie the slices flat on the baking tray. Using your thumbs and forefingers, pinch each slice gently, so you push the centres up a little, like a rosebud. Leave in a warm place for 15 minutes to rise.

Bake for 25 minutes until golden and fragrant. Transfer to a wire rack to cool for a few minutes before serving,

Makes 8

Tsoureki

These days you can buy tsoureki in pastry shops all through the year, but in Greek villages the making of tsoureki is still a special tradition reserved for the Thursday before Easter. Tsoureki is a rich, buttery brioche flavoured with masticha and mahlep and after the strict vegan diet that many people observe during Lent, it is greatly anticipated as celebration food. Waiting until after the Easter Mass is finished before indulging can often be almost too much to bear – especially when the tsoureki is fresh out of the oven, and still warm and fragrant.

I always make my tsoureki on Easter Saturday so it is still very fresh on Easter Sunday. And I have been known to sneak in a taste before the appointed time, justifying my weakness by saying that the cook needs to know that a dish is successful before offering it to others.

If you have an electric mixer with a dough hook then tsoureki is much easier to make. Mastic, mahlep and orange flower water are all available from Greek supermarkets or delicatessens.

....

40 g (1 ½ oz) dried yeast
325 g (11 ½ oz) sugar
190 ml (6 ½ oz) warm milk
1 kg (2 lb 3 oz) plain (all-purpose) flour
½ teaspoon salt
zest of 1 orange
1 tablespoon ground mastic

2 teaspoons ground mahlep
6 eggs, lightly beaten
2 teaspoons orange flower water
350 g (12½ oz) unsalted butter, softened
1 extra egg for glazing
50 g (1¾ oz) flaked almonds

Dissolve the yeast and 1 tablespoon of the sugar in the warm milk and leave in a warm place for about 10 minutes until it starts to froth up.

Sift the flour and salt into a large mixing bowl. Add the rest of the sugar with the orange zest, mastic and mahlep. Pour the frothy yeast into the flour and add the beaten eggs and orange flower water. Mix together well then knead for 10 minutes to form a smooth, elastic dough. You can do this by hand or with an electric mixer fitted with a dough hook. Shape the dough into a ball and place in an oiled bowl. Cover with plastic wrap and leave in a warm place for about 2 hours until the dough has doubled in size.

Punch the dough down then turn it out onto your work surface. Flatten it out into a disc, about 4 cm (1½ in) thick. Smear the surface with the softened butter then fold the sides in to enclose the butter. Place the dough in an electric mixer and knead until the butter is completely incorporated. This takes quite a while and the dough will become very sticky, but gradually it will come together.

Tip the dough out onto a work surface and knead with your hands until you have a smooth, glossy, manageable dough. Place in an oiled bowl and leave to rise overnight in a cool place – preferably in the fridge.

Preheat the oven to 180°C (350°F) and lightly grease a large baking tray.

Divide the dough into 9 even pieces, 3 for each loaf. Use your hands to roll each piece of dough into a thick sausage, about 25 cm (10 in) long. Lay 3 pieces side by side. Pinch them together at one end and weave into a plait. You can leave the loaf as a long plait or form it into a circle. Repeat with the remaining pieces of dough.

Place the 3 loaves onto the baking tray. Brush each with beaten egg and sprinkle with flaked almonds. Cover with a tea (dish) towel and leave in a warm place for 30 minutes to rise for a final time. Bake for 20 minutes then lower the heat to 160°C (320°F) and bake for a further 25 minutes until the loaves are fragrant and golden brown.

Makes 3 loaves

Filo pastry

Once you get the hang of making your own filo pastry, you'll never go back to using the shop-bought kind. The method is simple, but you need time to rest the dough and strong shoulders to roll all the little balls. But it is well worth the effort.

The quantities below are enough to make 6 x 40 cm (16 in) round sheets of pastry, sufficient for a large pie, sweet or savoury.

500 g (1 lb 2 oz) plain (all-purpose) flour, sifted
1 egg
1 teaspoon vinegar

1 tablespoon olive oil
200 ml (7 fl oz) cold water
250 g (9 oz) butter, melted

Combine the flour, egg, vinegar, olive oil and water in a food processor and whiz to form a ball. Wrap with plastic wrap and refrigerate for 1 hour.

Cut the pastry into 6 even portions and roll each into a thick sausage shape. Cut each sausage into 5, making a total of 30 little balls. Use a rolling pin to roll each little ball into a thin 15 cm (6 in) round. As you roll, stack the rounds on plates in groups of 5 brushing melted butter between each round. Cover each plate with plastic wrap and refrigerate until you have rolled out all the dough.

Starting with the first plate, lift the stack of pastry rounds onto your work surface and roll them out together to form a 40 cm (16 in) round. Continue with the remaining plates, until you have 6 round sheets of filo. If not using immediately, roll each sheet of filo in plastic wrap and refrigerate or freeze. Otherwise, continue according to each specific recipe.

Makes 6 pastry sheets

Pastourmopita

Pastourmas is cured beef with a spicy paprika crust, and it is available from Greek or Turkish delicatessens. Pastourmas can be sliced paper thin and served on its own as a cold meat appetiser. In this recipe it is cooked in a pie with filo pastry, cheese and eggs and cut into squares. Serve it as a tasty lunch dish or as a part of a mezze platter.

Emek yufka is handmade filo pastry, which is also available from Greek or Turkish delicatessens or supermarkets. If you can't find emek yufka, then use regular filo pastry.

....

200 g (7 oz) butter, melted
3 eggs
125 ml (4 fl oz) cream (whipping)
200 g (7 oz) feta cheese
100 g (3 ½ oz) ricotta

½ teaspoon freshly ground black pepper
dash of Tabasco
400 g (14 oz) emek yufka
300 g (10 ½ oz) pastourmas, finely sliced

Preheat the oven to 180°C (350°F). Brush a 23 cm x 30 cm x 5 cm (9 in x 12 in x 2 in) baking tray generously with melted butter.

To make the filling, whisk together the eggs and cream, then crumble in the feta and ricotta and stir to combine. Season with pepper and a generous dash of Tabasco.

Cut the pastry sheets into rectangles to fit the inside the buttered tray. Layer in 4 sheets of pastry, brushing each with a little melted butter. Cover with a layer of pastourma then pour in the filling. Cover with another layer of pastourma, then another four sheets of pastry. Again, brush each pastry sheet with a little melted butter. Refrigerate for 20 minutes then cut carefully into 5 cm x 3 cm (2 in x 1¼ in) rectangles.

Bake for 1 hour, until golden and puffed up. Serve at room temperature.

Makes about 20 squares

Spanakotiropita

In Kosta's village there is a great deal of rivalry among the women as to who makes the best spanakotiropita. I believe the secret is in the ratio of pastry to filling, and in the quality of the butter. There must be enough filling to provide moisture, balance of flavours and lightness, or the pie will be heavy and not as interesting. The taste of the butter is of utmost importance for a fresh, sweet pastry. Although this isn't a problem in Australia, it can be hard to achieve in Greece where fresh butter is not readily available, especially in small villages. Many women substitute margarine or Vitam (which is made from corn oil), but in my view this spoils the flavour of the pita and is a travesty, given the amount of work involved.

You can use the recipe for Filo Pastry on page 190, or good quality emek yufka, which is a commercially available handmade filo, available from Greek or Turkish delicatessens or supermarkets.

....

300 g (10 ½ oz) unsalted butter, melted
750 g (1 lb 10 oz) spinach leaves, washed and
    drained
2 tablespoons extra virgin olive oil
freshly ground black pepper

6 eggs
450 g (1 lb) feta cheese
dash of Tabasco
6 sheets Filo Pastry (page 190)
    or 400 g (14 oz) emek yufka

Brush a 4 cm deep x 30 cm (1 ½ in deep x 12 in) round baking tray generously with melted butter.

To make the filling, in a large saucepan wilt the spinach with the oil and pepper over a medium heat.

Whisk the eggs in a large mixing bowl. Crumble in the feta and season with more black pepper and a dash of Tabasco.

If using handmade filo pastry, trim the pastry, so that it is just a little bigger than the tray. Layer in 2 sheets of pastry, brushing each with a little melted butter. Spread on half the spinach and top with half the cheese filling. Cover with another sheet of pastry and brush with a little more melted butter. Spread on the remaining spinach and cheese filling then top with the remaining 3 pastry sheets, buttering as you go. Fold the pastry edges in and down the sides of the tin, so as to neatly enclose the filling.

If using emek yufka, cut each sheet into quarters. Lay 4 quarters in the base of the buttered baking tray, overlapping them in the centre of the tray and up the sides, with a 2 cm (¾ in) overhang. Layer on another 4 quarters, buttering as you go. Spread on half the spinach and top with half the cheese filling. Cover with another 4 quarters of emek yufka and brush with a little more melted butter. Spread on the remaining spinach and cheese filling then top with 4 more quarters of pastry. Fold the edges of the pastry in and down the sides of the tin, so as to neatly enclose the filling.

Brush the top of the pie with more melted butter, being especially careful not to brush on any white milk solids, as they will burn and look unsightly.

Refrigerate the spanakotiropita for 10 minutes while you preheat the oven to 180°C (350°F). Use a sharp knife to cut into 12 portions then bake for 50 minutes. Check the spanakotiropita then reduce the heat to 170°C (340°F) and bake for a further 10 minutes. The pie should puff up in the centre and be a lovely deep golden colour.

Serves 12

....

Our parallel lives

Running a small family restaurant can be relentless. Our summer season is short but intense and it's never easy to recruit enough staff to work for such a short period, so all family members are required to work long hours without any days off. We all look forward to having a long break in the winter months and most years we have managed a holiday in Greece in the family house in the village. Our boys spent much of their childhood with their cousins in Greece, riding their bikes around the village, going to the village school and, naturally, speaking Greek fluently from a young age.

In Lorne, as babies, Strato and Alex spent many hours in a playpen on the kitchen floor at the restaurant, playing with wooden spoons and saucepan lids, or riding their little plastic tractors around the dining room between the tables. Strato would often just lie down and fall asleep anywhere whenever he felt tired. We would find him asleep on a shelf in the larder with a bag of onions or potatoes as a pillow. At other times he'd tuck himself into a corner of the waiters' station in the dining room – a tiny sleeping body, oblivious to all the restaurant noise around him.

The boys also managed to do damage at the worst possible times. We used to store desserts in a fridge underneath the bar in the dining room. Kosta would make chocolate mousse in individual bowls and place them carefully on a tray in the fridge, only to discover just before service that little fingers had taken a scoop out of every single serve.

From a very young age our sons learnt to work in the restaurant: they could peel garlic, potatoes, carrots, shell peas, polish cutlery and wine glasses, and set the tables. For many years, before leaving for school in the morning, they set up the restaurant and carried tables and chairs out onto the footpath. In due course, while in their late teens, all three boys became skilled waiters. They had always been in the public eye and had developed confidence and social skills at a young age, so dealing with customers was second nature to them.

The other obvious advantage for children who grow up in a family restaurant is that they learn to eat and enjoy a wide range of foods. We never had to encourage our boys to eat. They were given whatever we were eating, as a matter of course. As small babies they loved offal (variety meats) – in particular, poached lamb's brains with parsley sauce – but most of all, like children everywhere, they loved the sweet things of life. Yiayia would make them poached fruits, depending on what was in season, and always had a bowl of stewed apricots, peaches or plums in her fridge. They loved to make little jam tarts and apple pies out of pieces of left-over pastry in the restaurant kitchen. And somehow, they were never far away when there was a pudding bowl to be scraped clean, ice cream churning or cakes coming out of the oven.

Desserts

Although we often think of Greek desserts as being sweet, syrupy things such as baklava, ravani and patzavoura, these sweets are generally not eaten after a meal. Instead they are eaten in the late afternoon when friends drop in, or when we go out for a volta – an evening stroll with friends to a coffee shop.

In Greece, the evening meal is eaten late – sometimes as late as midnight – and is generally finished with a plate of seasonal fresh fruit. In summer, this will probably be a slice of peponi (a green melon similar to honeydew) or a thick slice of watermelon, straight from the fridge, or perhaps a bowl of plump, black cherries. Autumn brings some of my favourite fruits, figs and grapes, and even in winter there are apples and pears.

Back in Australia at A la Grecque I love incorporating fruit into our desserts. In the summer, some of the most popular desserts are slow-roasted stone fruits, such as nectarines, peaches or plums. The slow cooking evaporates some of the juices and intensifies the flavour beautifully. We serve them simply, with yoghurt, cream and brown sugar.

Many fruits make wonderful tarts and are especially good when served with custard. One of my favourite combinations is fig, prune and mascarpone. This tart is very elegant, the custard stays soft and melting and the fruit steeped in port has a wonderful flavour. Another simple yet effective way of transforming fresh or poached fruit into a special dessert is to serve it with custard, mascarpone or ice cream and a sweet, buttery sablé biscuit (cookie).

Grapes can be wonderful cooked into a tarte tatin, especially when combined with ripe figs. And nothing can beat them when served fresh with a slice of creamy feta cheese. When figs are abundant I like to poach them in amaretto syrup to serve with almond cake. They are also a taste sensation eaten straight from the tree. As soon as they begin to droop, soft and heavy on the branches, they should be picked and eaten immediately. Once the skin is peeled back the flesh inside is like jam – purple, moist and sweet.

One of my favourite autumn fruits is the quince. At home in Lorne, when the nights start to get cold, we light our wood-burning stove and put a dish of quinces in the oven to bake with some honey and butter. They can be eaten warm with lots of custard and pure cream, baked into a tart or even added to a casserole of braised pork.

Almonds, walnuts, lemon and semolina feature in many Greek desserts. The nuts add texture and a delicious toasted flavour to many cakes or sweets that are made with semolina and soaked in lemony syrup. Halva semolina was Yiayia's speciality and was greatly loved by the children.

Another of Yiayia's favourite recipes was pashka. I believe that she was given the recipe by her koumbara (maid-of-honour), who brought it to Greece when she migrated there from Russia many decades ago. Pashka is the perfect celebration dessert. It is a delicious ricotta custard, flavoured with fruit, nuts and rosewater, and it can be dressed up with violets and served in a stemmed glass for a special occasion.

At A la Grecque we make all of our own ice creams. There are endless possibilities when one has a good ice cream machine. Most fruits make wonderful sorbets and ice creams, while chocolate is a perennial favourite. I like to add a little brandy to my chocolate ice cream, which makes it smooth, creamy and rich. It is delicious served just on its own, but can be teamed with fruit, nuts, biscuits or a tart to make a stunning dessert.

Slow-roasted nectarines with yoghurt, cream and brown sugar

This is a simple yet very effective dessert. Slow-roasting the nectarines intensifies their flavour by evaporating some of the liquid in the fruit. The yoghurt, cream and brown sugar are creamy, but with a sweet edge.

Feel free to substitute peaches or plums, depending on what is most readily available.

2 kg (4 lb 6 oz) nectarines, halved and stones removed
300 ml (10 fl oz) cream (whipping)

400 ml (13½ fl oz) plain yoghurt
150 g (5½ oz) brown sugar

Heat the oven to 160°C (320°F). Line a baking tray with baking paper.

Lay the nectarines in the baking tray, cut sides up. Bake for 1½–2 hours. The nectarines should be soft and caramelised on top but not disintegrating. Lift them carefully into a bowl and leave to cool.

Whip the cream to form soft peaks and gently fold it into the yoghurt. Spoon into a shallow dish and sprinkle with brown sugar. Leave in the fridge for at least 2 hours, and preferably 4, so that the sugar melts over the yoghurt cream.

Serve 3 or 4 nectarine halves in each bowl and top with a generous spoonful of yoghurt cream, making sure each person gets some of the brown sugar topping.

Serves 8

Slow-roasted plums with mascarpone cream, blackcurrant sauce and sablé biscuit

This dessert can be made with any variety of stone fruit and many variations of sauce and filling. For instance, try serving roasted peaches with vanilla ice cream and raspberries or baked quinces with lemon curd ice cream and Seville orange marmalade thinned into a sauce.

1 kg (2 lb 3 oz) vanilla plums (large black-skinned plums with yellow flesh)
2 cups blackcurrants
200 g (7 oz) caster (superfine) sugar
100 ml (3½ fl oz) Cassis (blackcurrant liqueur)
12 Sablé Biscuits (page 236)
icing (confectioners') sugar to serve

Mascarpone cream
200 g (7 oz) mascarpone cheese
200 g (7 oz) crème fraîche
½ teaspoon vanilla essence
50 g (1¾ oz) icing (confectioners') sugar

Heat the oven to 160°C (320°F). Line a baking tray with baking paper.

Cut the plums in half and remove the stone. Lay the plums in the baking tray, cut side up. Bake for 1½ hours. The plums should be soft and caramelised on top but not disintegrating. Lift them carefully into a bowl and leave to cool.

Combine the blackcurrants and sugar in a heavy-based saucepan and heat gently for about 15 minutes until the sugar dissolves in the juice. Remove from the heat and leave to cool. Tip into a food processor and whiz to a purée. Strain through a fine sieve then stir in the Cassis.

To make the mascarpone cream, put the mascarpone in a mixing bowl and whisk to slacken it. Add the remaining ingredients and continue whisking until it thickens to form a thick cream.

To serve, place a sablé biscuit (cookie) in the middle of each dessert plate and top with a spoonful of mascarpone cream. Top with another biscuit. Arrange a couple of roasted plums around the biscuit and drizzle with blackcurrant sauce. Dust with icing sugar and serve.

Serves 6

Peaches poached in lemon syrup

450 g (1 lb) sugar
300 ml (10 fl oz) lemon juice

rind of 1 lemon, julienned
6 ripe peaches

Combine the sugar, lemon juice and rind in a heavy-based saucepan and heat gently until the sugar has completely dissolved. Increase the heat and bring to the boil. Drop the peaches into the boiling syrup then cover the surface with a circle of baking paper. Simmer gently for 5 minutes then remove from the heat and leave to cool.

Serves 6

Fig, prune and mascarpone tart

This sweet pastry is easy to work with and ideal for making all kinds of fruit or custard tarts. Remember the cardinal rule when making pastry is that the less you work it the better. And for most tarts the pastry shell will need to be blind baked (pre-cooked) before adding the filling of your choice.

Although this tart is not traditionally Greek, it is a favourite of mine as I think figs and prunes go together so well. They are rich and dense and make beautiful desserts. This tart can also be served for afternoon tea.

....

Sweet shortcrust pastry
330 g (11 ½ oz) plain (all-purpose) flour
110 g (4 oz) caster (superfine) sugar
220 g (8 oz) unsalted butter, chilled and
    roughly diced
4 egg yolks

6 dried figs, sliced
12 pitted prunes
125 ml (4 fl oz) port
3 eggs
80 g (2¾ oz) caster (superfine) sugar
250 g (9 oz) mascarpone
250 ml (8 ½ fl oz) cream (whipping)

Heat the oven to 180°C (350°F) and grease a 23 cm (9 in) loose-based tart tin.

To make the pastry, place the flour and sugar in the bowl of a food processor and whiz to combine.

Add the butter and whiz until the mixture looks like breadcrumbs. Add the egg yolks and whiz until the pastry just comes together to form a ball. Do not overwork. Wrap in plastic wrap and rest in the refrigerator for at least 1 hour before use.

Dust the prepared tart tin lightly with flour. Roll the pastry out to 5 mm (¼ in) thick, then lift it onto the tin and gently ease into the edges and up the sides, leaving an overhang of about 2 cm (¾ in). Refrigerate for 20 minutes.

Remove from the fridge and roll over the edges of the tin with a rolling pin to trim the edges neatly. Prick the pastry base with a fork then line with baking paper and baking beans (dried beans or chickpeas/garbanzo beans). Bake for 20 minutes then remove the paper and beans and cook for a further 10 minutes, or until the pastry is just cooked.

To prepare the filling, combine the figs, prunes and port in a heavy-based saucepan and simmer gently until the fruit is soft and all the liquid has been absorbed. Remove from the heat and allow to cool. Spoon the mixture evenly into the pre-baked tart shell.

In an electric mixer, whisk the eggs until light and fluffy. Whisk in the sugar, followed by the mascarpone and then the cream. Pour the mixture over the fruit in the tart tin and bake for 45–50 minutes, until set and golden.

Serves 10

....

Chocolate tarts

Whenever we put this tart on the menu at A la Grecque, it is so popular that we can barely keep up with making it!

75 g (2½ oz) dark cooking chocolate
6 egg yolks
125 g (4 oz) caster (superfine) sugar
60 g (2 oz) honey
140 g (5 oz) unsalted butter
75 g (2½ oz) cocoa powder
225 ml (8 oz) cream (whipping), whipped
   to soft peaks

6 x 8 cm (3 in) pre-baked Sweet Shortcrust Pastry
   tart shells (Sweet Shortcrust Pastry page 205)

Ganache
100 g (3½ oz) dark cooking chocolate
50 ml (1¾ fl oz) cream (whipping)

Half-fill a large saucepan with water and bring to the boil. Place the chocolate in a bowl and sit on top of the saucepan of boiling water, making sure the water doesn't touch the bowl. (A stainless steel bowl is best, as it is a good conductor of heat.) Heat until the chocolate has dissolved, then stir gently.

In another stainless steel bowl, whisk the egg yolks with the sugar and honey. Stir in the melted chocolate then sit on top of the saucepan of boiling water. Cook, stirring continuously with a wooden spoon, until the temperature reaches 83°C (180°F). If you don't have a thermometer, the custard should be thick enough to coat the back of the spoon. Remove from the heat and leave to cool.

In an electric mixer, beat the butter with the cocoa powder until well combined. With the motor running, pour in the cooled chocolate mixture and beat until combined.

Fold in the whipped cream then pour the filling into the pre-baked pastry shells and refrigerate until cold before icing.

To make the ganache, combine the chocolate and cream in a stainless steel bowl and melt over a saucepan of boiling water. When melted, stir to combine and ice the tarts, spreading it on to form a smooth layer.

Makes 6

Baked filo with yoghurt custard and lemon syrup
Patzavoura

This translates into English as 'mop head', as Greek mops look like pleated strips of fabric, and this is the effect of the filo pastry in this dessert. The pastry is topped with custard, baked and then drenched with syrup. It is very sweet, so add plenty of lemon juice to the syrup.

Emek yufka is handmade filo pastry, which is available from Greek or Turkish delicatessens or supermarkets. If you can't find emek yufka, then use regular filo pastry – but the texture of the dessert will be different.

15 g (½ oz) butter, melted
6 eggs
250 g (9 oz) caster (superfine) sugar
250 g (9 oz) plain yoghurt
1 teaspoon baking powder
125 ml (4 fl oz) vegetable oil
900 g (2 lb) emek yufka

Syrup
250 g (9 oz) sugar
125 ml (4 fl oz) water
juice and zest of 1 lemon

Preheat the oven to 180°C (350°F). Brush a 30 cm (12 in) diameter baking dish with the melted butter.

Whisk the eggs with the sugar until pale and creamy. Add the yoghurt, baking powder and oil and whisk together well.

Gather sheets of emuk yufka into pleats and fit them into the baking dish until the base is completely covered. Pour on the custard and bake for 35 minutes until the custard is set and golden brown.

While the tart is baking, make the syrup. Combine the sugar, water, lemon juice and zest in a heavy-based saucepan. Heat gently to dissolve the sugar then increase the heat and bring to the boil. Simmer for 5 minutes then remove from the heat and leave to cool slightly.

Pour the warm syrup over the custard and pastry while still warm. Cut into portions while still in the dish. Refrigerate and serve cold.

Makes about 24 pieces

Semolina halvas

This Greek sweet was Yiayia's speciality. Even at the age of ninety she often insisted on making halvas as a treat for my son Dominic. That is to say, she would start making it and then get tired of all the stirring. I would then be 'allowed' to finish making it under her watchful eye!

Although it can be eaten cold, halvas is delicious eaten warm and smothered in ground cinnamon.

200 g (7 oz) unsalted butter
400 g (14 oz) coarse semolina
600 g (1 lb 5 oz) caster (superfine) sugar
1.5 litres (51 fl oz) cold water

zest of 1 orange
200 g (7 oz) toasted walnuts
ground cinnamon

Melt the butter in a large heavy-based saucepan. Add the semolina and sugar and cook over a medium heat for about 15 minutes, stirring continuously with a wooden spoon, until is the mixture is golden brown.

Remove from the heat and add the water and orange zest. Put the pot back onto medium heat and stir constantly for 15–20 minutes until the mixture is thick and comes away from the sides of the saucepan in a cohesive mass. Pour into a buttered shallow dish. Decorate with walnuts and sprinkle generously with cinnamon. Cool and cut into diamond shapes to serve. Warm slightly to serve, as the butter will set hard if refrigerated.

Serves 12

Almond cake with moscato jelly and amaretto figs

This is a beautifully moist, subtly flavoured almond cake that is equally good served as a dessert or for afternoon tea. The recipe has very little flour as the marzipan binds the mixture. It keeps well in an airtight container.

....

Almond marzipan cake
250 g (9 oz) unsalted butter
110 g (4 oz) caster (superfine) sugar
zest of 1 lemon and 1 orange
230 g (8 oz) marzipan, chopped
4 eggs
50 g (1¾ oz) plain (all-purpose) flour
¼ teaspoon baking powder
80 g (2¾ oz) flaked almonds

Moscato jelly
500 ml (17 fl oz) moscato
1 tablespoon sugar
3 sheets gelatine

Amaretto figs
250 g (9 oz) sugar
125 ml (4 fl oz) water
400 g (14 oz) ripe figs
100 ml (3½ fl oz) amaretto

Preheat your oven to 180°C (350°F) and grease and line a 23 cm (9 in) spring-form cake tin.

Combine the butter and sugar in an electric mixer and beat until pale and fluffy. Add the citrus zest, then the marzipan, beating well until the marzipan is completely incorporated.

Add the eggs one at a time, beating well after each addition. Sift the flour and baking powder together and fold into the cake mixture. Spoon into the cake tin and sprinkle the surface with flaked almonds. Bake for 45 minutes, or until cooked. Remove from the oven and leave to cool in the tin.

To make the jelly, combine the moscato and sugar in a heavy-based saucepan and heat gently until the sugar has completely dissolved. Soak the gelatine sheets in cold water for 2 minutes until soft. Remove the sheets from the water and squeeze to remove the excess water. Add to the hot moscato and stir to dissolve completely. Divide the jelly mixture evenly among 8 x 100 ml (3½ fl oz) dariole (cylindrical) moulds and refrigerate for about 2 hours until set.

To make the amaretto figs, combine the sugar and water in a heavy-based saucepan and heat gently until the sugar has completely dissolved. Increase the heat and simmer for 5 minutes to make a syrup. Drop the figs into the boiling syrup then cover the surface with a circle of baking paper. Remove from the heat and leave to cool before stirring in the amaretto.

When ready to serve, dip the jelly moulds briefly in hot water and turn out onto serving plates. Serve with a slice of the almond cake and a poached fig.

Serves 10

....

Vanilla ice cream

Use this recipe as a base mix for making any number of ice creams, simply by adding different flavours and fruits. Add 500 ml (17 fl oz) Lemon Curd (page 218), for instance, to make a delcious lemon ice cream. Alternatively, fold in any variety of fresh or frozen berries or crushed, toasted hazelnuts and Frangelico instead of kirsch.

If you are interested in making your own ice creams regularly at home, then I suggest you invest in a sugar thermometer and an ice cream machine. A thermometer takes the guesswork out of making the base mixture (and is invaluable in all sorts of other desserts as well). A machine makes the whole business of churning so much easier, and you really do get a smoother, richer ice cream as a result.

500 ml (17 fl oz) milk
500 ml (17 fl oz) cream (whipping)
1 vanilla pod

12 egg yolks
300 g (10 ½ oz) caster (superfine) sugar
60 ml (2 fl oz) kirsch

Combine the milk and cream in a heavy-based saucepan. Split the vanilla pod and scrape the seeds into the pan. Add the pod as well and bring to a simmer.

Half-fill another large saucepan with water and bring to the boil. Whisk the egg yolks with the sugar in a bowl until pale and creamy. (A stainless steel bowl is best, as it is a good conductor of heat.) Slowly pour the hot milk and cream onto the egg mixture, whisking continuously. Sit the bowl on top of the saucepan of boiling water, making sure the water doesn't touch the bowl. Cook, stirring continuously with a wooden spoon, until the temperature reaches 83°C (180°F). If you don't have a thermometer, the custard should be thick enough to coat the back of the spoon.

Remove from the heat and strain through a fine sieve. (The vanilla pod can be rinsed, dried and used to perfume a jar of sugar.) Allow the custard to cool then stir in the kirsch. When ready to churn, tip into an ice cream machine and churn according to the manufacturer's instructions. Transfer to a plastic container and freeze, it will keep for up to a week but may become icy if kept any longer.

Makes 1.5 litres (51 fl oz)

Coconut ice cream

This ice cream goes beautifully with fresh mango or pineapple or even just with a ginger biscuit (cookie). Scoop into balls and roll them in extra toasted shredded coconut for an amazing presentation.

....

500 ml (17 fl oz) coconut cream
500 ml (17 fl oz) cream (whipping)
12 egg yolks

200 g (7 oz) caster (superfine) sugar
60 ml (2 fl oz) Malibu
150 g (5½ oz) toasted shredded coconut

Follow the method described for making Vanilla Ice Cream (opposite), substituting coconut cream for the milk and Malibu for the kirsch. Towards the end of the churning, add the toasted coconut.

Transfer to a plastic container and freeze. It will keep for up to a week but may become icy if kept any longer.

Makes 1.5 litres (51 fl oz)

Chocolate ice cream

A rich, dark ice cream that's made with sugar syrup instead of milk. The brandy prevents it from becoming icy in the freezer.

....

250 g (9 oz) caster (superfine) sugar
160 ml (5 ½ fl oz) water
500 g (1 lb 2 oz) dark cooking chocolate
100 g (3 ½ oz) cocoa powder

200 ml (7 fl oz) brandy
14 egg yolks
1.5 litres (51 fl oz) cream (whipping)

Put the sugar and water in a heavy-based saucepan and heat gently to dissolve. Increase the heat and simmer for 5 minutes to make a syrup. Remove from the heat and allow to cool.

Half-fill another large saucepan with water and bring to the boil. Combine the chocolate, cocoa and brandy in a bowl and sit on top of the saucepan of boiling water, making sure the water doesn't touch the bowl. (A stainless steel bowl is best, as it is a good conductor of heat.) Heat until the chocolate has melted, then stir gently to combine. Set the bowl aside.

In a different stainless steel bowl, whisk the egg yolks with the sugar syrup and sit the bowl on top of the boiling water, making sure the water doesn't touch the bowl. Cook, stirring continuously with a wooden spoon, until the temperature reaches 83°C (180°F). If you don't have a thermometer, the custard should be thick enough to coat the back of the spoon.

Remove from the heat and stir in the melted chocolate mixture. Stir in the cream and whisk to combine. Tip into an ice cream machine and churn according to the manufacturer's instructions. Transfer to a plastic container and freeze for up to a week.

Makes 2 litres (68 fl oz)

Lemon curd

We all love lemon curd on toast for breakfast, but it is also invaluable in the dessert world. It can be added to a basic vanilla ice cream, mix and churned to make a delicious lemon ice cream; served on top of ice cream, yoghurt or hotcakes; combined with passionfruit for layering in a sponge cake or between sablé biscuits (cookies); or served alongside baked quinces or rhubarb.

....

6 eggs
450 g (1 lb) caster (superfine) sugar
juice of 6 lemons and finely grated zest
   of 4 lemons
125 g (4 oz) unsalted butter, chopped

Half-fill a large saucepan with water and bring to the boil. Whisk the eggs with the sugar, lemon juice and zest in a bowl until pale and creamy. (A stainless steel bowl is best, as it is a good conductor of heat.) Sit the bowl on top of the saucepan of boiling water, making sure the water doesn't touch the bowl. Add the pieces of butter and cook, stirring with a wooden spoon. If you don't stir continuously at first, you may find flecks of cooked egg whites appear in the curd. However once the mixture begins to thicken and the egg is cooked, you can stir less frequently until it reaches the desired consistency.

Remove from the heat and allow to cool. Transfer to sterilised jars and seal. Store in the fridge for up to 2 weeks.

Makes 1 litre (34 fl oz)

Seville orange custard

Seville oranges are tart and sour and are probably best known for making marmalade, but their intense orange flavour makes them ideal for all sorts of desserts, such as this custard. I love to use it as an accompaniment to tarts and cakes, such as the Lemon Yoghurt Cake on page 228. But it's just as delicious eaten on its own, or poured over a scoop of ice cream.

   The quantities make about 1.5 litres (51 fl oz), but can be halved if you prefer.

....

900 ml (30½ fl oz) cream (whipping)
zest and juice of 2 large Seville oranges
220 g (8 oz) caster (superfine) sugar
8 egg yolks
4 tablespoons Cointreau

Follow the method for making Vanilla Ice Cream (page 214), adding the orange zest and juice to the eggs and sugar before whisking together, and substituting Cointreau for the kirsch.

Instead of freezing, refrigerate the custard. It will keep for 2–3 days.

Makes about 1.5 litres (51 fl oz)

Pashka

A celebratory Easter dessert that looks stunning, especially when decorated with fresh or crystallised violets and served in an attractive wine glass or glass dish.

4 egg yolks
200 g (7 oz) caster (superfine) sugar
250 ml (8½ fl oz) cream (whipping)
½ vanilla pod
750 g (1 lb 10 oz) ricotta
200 g (7 oz) unsalted butter, softened
125 g (4 oz) raisins

150 g (5½ oz) glacé apricots, finely chopped
150 g (5½ oz) glacé figs, finely chopped
150 g (5½ oz) candied orange peel, finely chopped
150 g (5½ oz) flaked almonds, toasted
2 teaspoons rosewater
2 teaspoons finely grated orange zest
fresh or crystallised violets (optional) to serve

Combine the egg yolks and sugar in a stainless steel mixing bowl and whisk until pale and creamy.

Pour the cream into a heavy-based saucepan. Split the piece of vanilla pod and scrape the seeds into the pan. Add the pod as well and bring to the boil. Remove from the heat, remove the vanilla pod and pour onto the eggs and sugar, whisking all the time.

Half-fill another large saucepan with water and bring to the boil. Sit the bowl on top of the saucepan of boiling water, making sure the water doesn't touch the bowl. Cook, stirring continuously with a wooden spoon, until the temperature reaches 83°C (180°F). If you don't have a thermometer, the custard should be thick enough to coat the back of the spoon.

In a different bowl, beat the ricotta with the softened butter. Slowly pour the hot custard onto the ricotta mixture, stirring until well combined. Fold in the chopped fruit, peel, nuts, rosewater and zest.

Spoon into individual moulds or serving glasses and refrigerate. Decorate with fresh or crystallised violets, if using, and serve.

Serves 12

Making yoghurt at home

I far prefer to make yoghurt from sheep's milk. It has a higher fat content than cow's milk, so it is thick and creamy – and, of course, very fattening! In Greece sheep's milk is readily available as many people keep sheep for both milk and meat and most village women make their own yoghurt and cheese. Here in Australia you may find it difficult to source sheep's milk, unless you breed your own sheep for milking or know a farmer who does. However, it is still worth making your own yoghurt with cow's milk.

There are a number of very good yoghurts available commercially these days, but somehow home-made yoghurt is much nicer; mainly because it is less acidic and has a lighter, more delicate texture.

....

2 litres (68 fl oz) fresh sheep's milk

1 tablespoon sheep's milk yoghurt (the 'starter'), either purchased or kept from a previous home-made batch

Strain the milk through a piece of muslin (cheesecloth) to remove any impurities. Bring the milk to a boil in a large heavy-based saucepan. Then lower the heat to medium and simmer for at least 5 minutes. Pour the boiling milk into a large glass bowl and leave it to cool.

This is the critical part. The natural bacteria will only work within a range of 32°C–49°C (90°F–120°F); any cooler and they won't start to grow, any hotter and they will be destroyed. If you don't have a thermometer, then allow the milk to cool until you can hold your finger in the milk comfortably for 11 seconds, without it scalding you.

Put the yoghurt starter in a small bowl, then add a few tablespoons of the warm milk and stir until smooth. Pour it back into the warm milk and stir it in quickly so the milk doesn't cool too much more. Cover the bowl with a lid (a large plate or a tray will do), and wrap it up in an old woollen blanket. Leave it in a warm place for 3½ hours without disturbing. On a hot day, check the bowl after 3 hours to see if the yoghurt has set. On a cold day it may need more time. Don't leave it for too long or it will lose some of its sweetness and become a little sour.

Transfer the set yoghurt to the fridge where it will keep for up to 2 weeks. Use a spoonful as a starter to make a new batch.

Makes 2 litres (68 fl oz)

A piece of paradise

I grew up on a farm near Wangaratta in the north east of Victoria and as is the case for many on the land, we had a frugal country lifestyle. Lamb (or more often mutton) was on the menu every day, along with boiled vegetables; stewed fruit with custard was the standard dessert. My mother sewed all of our clothes, including our school uniforms, and each daughter had one good dress for church on Sundays.

After I married and became a mother I began to yearn for some land where I could keep chickens, grow vegetables and have a dog. I dragged poor Kosta all over the country looking at properties, ranging from vineyards to sheep stations. He was patient but definite and the answer was always no!

But after twenty-one years of living next door to our restaurant on the busy main street of Lorne, I learnt that a block of land was to be offered for sale just outside the town. My dream came true when we purchased 2.6 hectares (6½ acres) of relatively clear land and began to build our ideal home and garden. We sited the house on the top of a hill where it had sweeping views down to the sea and over the surrounding bushland. Building a new house was the opportunity for me to design the kitchen I'd always longed for, with space for baking, a marble bench for rolling pastry and a wood-fuelled stove where I could have soups simmering on the hob on a cold winter's day.

Starting a garden from scratch was challenging. We had to deal with clay soil, kangaroos and cockatoos, bush rats and a ceaseless, howling south-westerly wind. Chickens and ducks were my first priority. They provide a veritable wealth: eggs for the kitchen and manure for the garden. Next, we planted an orchard of fruit trees. Olives, chestnuts, hazelnuts and citrus trees followed – all battling the elements, but all surviving. For the kitchen garden we chose the obvious place, a relatively flat area close to the house, and over the years we have dug truckloads of manure, straw and sand into these beds. A permanent bed of asparagus bears the fruit of good preparation and patience, with metre- (3 feet-) deep trenches dug and filled with sand and manure before the corms were planted, and then three years of waiting to cut the first crop.

Ironically, it is at the stage of your life when you finally have the dream kitchen, a flourishing garden, an abundance of produce and the time to indulge yourself, that your children leave home and you find yourself cooking for two people. Lucky for us then, that we are able to use our excess eggs and garden produce in the restaurant. And just like the women in our village in Greece, I find myself making batches of jams and cakes, which are easily transported over to Melbourne to stock up the boys' pantries.

....

Living in such a beautiful environment, Kosta and I are reminded every single day how lucky we are to live and work in this piece of paradise. We love to get to the beach, every day if possible, for a walk or a swim. Kosta, the 'Spartan', braves the icy water all year around. I am not as brave, but on most summer mornings I do enjoy an invigorating swim before breakfast and work. To wake early on a bright summer day and be the only person in the water, or the first person on the beach, is always memorable. Even the drive to work along the Great Ocean Road is a pleasure that not many people are lucky enough to experience as a part of their daily routine.

At A la Grecque we have tried to create a space where friends and customers feel comfortable and at home. We believe that our restaurant should be accessible to everyone and we aim to attract a broad range of patrons. Our philosophy is based on three factors which we feel are fundamental to a successful dining experience: excellent food, excellent service and value for money. Naturally there are a hundred other details which must also be attended to, but these three stand out as the essential ingredients of success.

Kosta and I spend most of our days at the restaurant, and we treat it as an extension of our home, offering food, wine and hospitality as we would in our own dining room. We really enjoy being able to share a table with friends at any time of the day or evening. Sometimes for a meal, at other times just for a coffee and a piece of hazelnut cake or some kourabiedes, or for a glass of wine and a cheeseplate with a slice of polenta, pine nut and dried fruit cake.

Afternoon tea

It is common for Greek people to arrange to meet friends in the late afternoon at a kafeteria (coffee shop) where they will sit for hours over a frappé or an ice cream.

Greeks also love to visit friends and relatives at the weekends. They would never dream of arriving empty-handed and usually take a beautifully wrapped box of biscuits (cookies) or syrupy cakes bought from a zacharoplasteia (confectionery shop). Village women still make cakes and koulourakia at home, and these are offered when friends call in for coffee. Most syrupy cakes such as baklava, kataifi and galaktoboureko are very sweet and are always served with a glass of iced water.

A special day in the village is All Souls Day, when every housewife makes something to be taken out of the house into the street where it is offered to friends and neighbours in remembrance of deceased relatives. Usually this offering will be loukoumades (deep-fried pastries drenched in syrup), or pissies (deep-fried mini-pancakes smothered in sugar), but some local women also make savoury pastries, such as tiropita or spanakotiropita. I like to make walnut biscotti, as they are perfect with tea or coffee for breakfast or for afternoon tea. Kourabiedes are another favourite, which I make all year round at A la Grecque. They are basically a buttery shortbread biscuit (cookie), but the addition of toasted almonds and a drenching of icing (confectioners') sugar makes them sweet and crumbly — wonderful with a cup of tea.

Lemon yoghurt cake

Lemon is one of my favourite flavours, especially when teamed with yoghurt. I find that the tang of the acid in both the lemon and yoghurt blends with sugar in cakes or desserts to make a creamy, sweet–sour combination that stimulates the palate without being too sweet.

125 g (4 oz) unsalted butter
220 g (8 oz) caster (superfine) sugar
2 eggs
250 ml (8 ½ fl oz) thick plain yoghurt
3 tablespoons lemon juice
1 tablespoon lemon zest
430 g (15 oz) self-raising flour
½ teaspoon bicarbonate of soda (baking soda)

Syrup
125 g (4 oz) sugar
125 ml (4 fl oz) water
3 tablespoons lemon juice
rind of 1 lemon, julienned
créme fraîche, to serve

Preheat the oven to 180°C (350°F) and grease and line a 23 cm (9 in) spring-form cake tin.

Combine the butter and sugar in an electric mixer and beat until pale and fluffy. Add the eggs one at a time, beating well after each addition then add the yoghurt, lemon juice and zest. Sift the flour and bicarb together and fold into the cake mixture. Bake for 45 minutes, or until cooked.

Make the syrup while the cake is baking. Combine the sugar, water, lemon juice and rind in a heavy-based saucepan. Heat gently to dissolve the sugar then increase the heat and bring to the boil. Simmer for 5 minutes to form a syrup then remove from the heat and pour over the hot cake while still in the tin. Leave to cool slightly and serve with crème fraîche.

Serves 10

Chocolate cake

You can make this cake entirely in a food processor. It is an excellent all-purpose cake that can be dressed up for special occasions. Slice it through the middle horizontally and fill it with jam, fresh berries, cream or serve it with Coffee Crème Anglaise (page 230) – whatever you fancy. Top with Ganache (page 206) or dust with cocoa powder.

....

250 g (9 oz) unsalted butter, melted
200 g (7 oz) caster (superfine) sugar
250 g (9 oz) good quality dark chocolate
250 ml (8 ½ fl oz) freshly made strong espresso coffee

2 eggs
2 teaspoons vanilla essence
200 g (7 oz) self-raising flour
50 g cocoa powder

Preheat the oven to 180°C (350°F) and grease and line a 23 cm (9 in) spring-form cake tin.

Combine the butter, sugar, chocolate and hot coffee in a food processor and whiz until the sugar has dissolved and chocolate has completely melted.

Add the eggs and vanilla and whiz briefly.

Sift the flour with the cocoa and add to the bowl. Whiz until smooth. Spoon the cake batter into the cake tin and bake for 40 minutes, or until cooked.

Serves 10

Hazelnut cake

Hazelnuts and brown sugar complement each other beautifully in this nutty cake. It also makes a wonderful dessert served with coffee and cognac.

....

300 g (10 ½ oz) brown sugar
240 g (8 ½ oz) plain (all-purpose) flour
130 g (4 ½ oz) unsalted butter, roughly chopped
240 ml (8 fl oz) cream (heavy/double)
2 eggs
1 teaspoon baking powder
200 g (7 oz) roasted hazelnuts, roughly chopped

Coffee crème anglaise
200 ml (7 fl oz) milk
200 ml (7 fl oz) cream (whipping)
150 ml (5 fl oz) very strong espresso coffee
5 egg yolks
200 g (7 oz) sugar
50 ml (1¾ fl oz) Kahlúa

Preheat the oven to 180°C (350°F) and grease and line a 23 cm (9 in) spring-form cake tin.

Combine the brown sugar and flour in a mixing bowl. Use your fingertips to rub in the butter until the mixture resembles breadcrumbs. Spread half the mixture into the bottom of the cake tin.

In a separate mixing bowl, whisk together the cream, eggs, and baking powder. Fold the remaining flour mixture in until thoroughly combined. Pour into the cake tin and scatter on the chopped hazelnuts. Bake for 40 minutes then remove the cake from the oven and cool on a wire rack.

To make the coffee crème anglaise, combine the milk, cream and coffee in a heavy-based saucepan and bring to the boil. Remove from the heat.

Half-fill another large saucepan with water and bring to the boil. Whisk the egg yolks with the sugar in a bowl until pale and creamy. (A stainless steel bowl, is best, as it is a good conductor of heat.) Slowly pour the hot milk onto the egg mixture, whisking continuously. Sit the bowl on top of the saucepan of boiling water, making sure the water doesn't touch the bowl. Cook, stirring continuously with a wooden spoon, until the temperature reaches 83°C (180°F). If you don't have a thermometer, the custard should be thick enough to coat the back of the spoon.

Remove from the heat and cool quickly in the refrigerator to prevent further cooking. When cold, stir in the Kahlúa.

Serve the cake with a generous amount of coffee crème anglaise.

Serves 8

BE CAREFUL,
THE NEXT PAGE
MAY BE ODD.

R J JULIA

BOOKSELLERS
"a great place to meet books"
768 Boston Post Road, Madison, CT 06443
203-245-3959   1-800-74-READS
~We're on Facebook~
Tweet us @rjjulia
www.rjjulia.com

Warm pear cake

Make this cake in the autumn when pears are at their best. It is a very moist cake and will keep well for a few days. Serve for afternoon tea, or as a dessert, with whipped cream and caramel sauce.

2 eggs
250 ml (8 ½ fl oz) corn oil
330 g (11 ½ oz) caster (superfine) sugar
1 tablespoon water
1 teaspoon vanilla essence
300 g (10 ½ oz) plain (all-purpose) flour
1 teaspoon bicarbonate of soda (baking soda)

2 teaspoons cinnamon
¼ teaspoon ground nutmeg
3 ripe pears, peeled, cored and sliced

Caramel sauce
250 g (9 oz) caster (superfine) sugar
250 ml (8 ½ fl oz) cream (whipping)

Preheat the oven to 180°C (350°F) and grease and line a 23 cm (9 in) spring-form cake tin.

Whisk the eggs with the oil until light and frothy. Add the sugar, water and vanilla, beating continuously.

Sift the flour with the bicarbonate of soda and the spices. Fold into the egg mixture. Stir in the pears then scrape the batter into the cake tin and bake for 1¼ hours.

While the cake is baking, make the caramel sauce. Heat the sugar in a heavy-based saucepan until it melts and turns a caramel brown. Remove the pan from the heat and carefully pour in the cream. It will spit and bubble up, so be careful not to burn yourself. Return the pan to a low heat and cook for about 5 minutes, stirring, until the sauce thickens.

Serve the warm pear cake with a generous amount of caramel sauce.

Serves 8

Polenta cake with pine nuts and dried fruit

This is a hearty cake that is lovely to serve with cheese for afternoon tea or supper. I often make it to take when we go camping. It makes an excellent sustaining breakfast in the absence of fresh bread or muesli and after a long day travelling or bush-walking it's a great reviver when served with a cup of tea. It keeps well.

850 ml (28 ½ fl oz) water
400 g (14 oz) polenta
1 teaspoon salt
3 tablespoons olive oil
60 g (2 oz) butter
2 eggs, lightly beaten
100 g (3 ½ oz) pine nuts, toasted, plus extra
   to decorate (optional)

150 g (5 oz) raisins
150 g (5 oz) dried figs, sliced
4 tablespoons raw (demerara) sugar
3 tablespoons fennel seeds
250 g (9 oz) plain (all-purpose) flour

Preheat the oven to 180°C (350°F) and grease and line a 23 cm (9 in) cake tin.

Bring the water to a boil in a heavy-based saucepan. Pour in the polenta in a thin stream, stirring all the time. Lower the heat to a simmer and add the salt and oil. Simmer for 15 minutes, stirring continuously. It will be very thick. Remove from the heat and stir in the butter. Add the eggs and stir them in well. Next, add the pine nuts, raisins, figs, sugar and fennel seeds and mix thoroughly. Sift on the flour and stir it in.

Spoon the mixture into the cake tin, then press it in smoothly with wet hands. Cover the top with some extra pine nuts if you wish. Bake for 40 minutes then remove from the oven and turn out of the tin while warm. Serve with Parmigiano Reggiano or gorgonzola.

Serves 12

Ravani

This cake is a local speciality from Kosta's village in Greece. This recipe makes a large 30 cm x 20 cm (12 in x 8 in) cake that will serve about 20 people. You can quite happily halve the quantities and make it in a 20 cm (8 in) spring-form cake tin.

When drenched with syrup it will be quite wet.

....

4 eggs
450 g (1 lb) caster (superfine) sugar
250 ml (8½ fl oz) yoghurt
1 teaspoon vanilla essence
450 g (1 lb oz) plain (all-purpose) flour
2 teaspoons baking powder
450 g (1 lb) fine semolina

Syrup
1 litre (34 fl oz) water
850 g (1 lb 14 oz) sugar
juice and zest of 1 lemon

Preheat the oven to 180°C (350°F) and grease a 30 cm x 20 cm (12 in x 8 in) ovenproof dish.

Combine the eggs and sugar in an electric mixer and beat until pale and creamy. Add the yoghurt and vanilla and beat gently until incorporated.

Sift the flour and baking powder together and fold into the egg mixture. Stir in the semolina. Spoon into the ovenproof dish and bake for 40 minutes, or until cooked.

While the cake is baking, make the syrup. Combine the sugar, water, lemon juice and zest in a heavy-based saucepan. Heat gently to dissolve the sugar then increase the heat and bring to the boil. Simmer for 30 minutes then remove from the heat and leave to cool slightly.

Cut the cake into 6 cm x 3 cm (2½ in x 1¼ in) portions while still in the dish. Pour the warm syrup over the warm cake. Serve with ice cream.

Serves 20

Sablé biscuits

Sablé biscuits (cookies) are delicious served with afternoon tea or coffee. Alternatively, they can be sandwiched with cream, custard or ice cream and served with fresh berries to make a quick and easy summer dessert.

....

330 g (11½) plain (all-purpose) flour
110 g (4 oz) icing (confectioners') sugar
220 g (8 oz) unsalted butter, chilled and
    roughly diced)
4 egg yolks

Grease and line a baking tray.

Place the flour and icing sugar in the bowl of a food processor and whiz to combine.

Add the butter and whiz until the mixture looks like breadcrumbs. Add the egg yolks and whiz until the pastry just comes together to form a ball. Do not overwork. Wrap with plastic wrap and rest in the refrigerator for at least 1 hour before use.

To make sablé biscuits, roll the pastry out to about 5 mm (¼ in) thick. Cut into circles with a 7.5 cm (3 in) pastry cutter and lift onto the baking tray. Refrigerate for 30 minutes while you preheat the oven to 180°C (350°F).

Bake for 15 minutes until the biscuits are crisp and pale gold. Transfer to a wire rack to cool before serving, or store in an airtight container.

Makes about 40

Semolina cake with ricotta, lemon curd and lemon syrup

Semolina is used frequently in Greek cooking, especially in desserts. It has a great texture and because it is absorbent it teams very well with syrups.

Syrup is another universal feature of Greek desserts and cakes because it adds moisture and softness. Although they are big consumers of milk, feta and yoghurt, Greeks have traditionally not eaten butter or cream in their diet. Instead they make liberal use of olive oil and a type of margarine made from corn oil. Many Greek cakes rely on syrup for a soft texture that might otherwise be achieved by a creamed butter and sugar base.

Although this cake is delicious as is, you can turn it into a very special dessert by accompanying it with Peaches Poached in Lemon Syrup (page 203).

....

Semolina cake
150 g (5½ oz) caster (superfine) sugar
5 eggs, separated
100 g (3½ oz) fine semolina
50 g (1¾ oz) ground almonds
pinch of salt
1 tablespoon Cointreau
1 tablespoon lemon juice
1 tablespoon grated lemon zest

Filling
150 g (5½ oz) ricotta
75 g (2½ oz) caster (superfine) sugar
150 ml (5 fl oz) cream (heavy/double)
½ cup Lemon Curd (page 218)

Lemon syrup
110 g (4 oz) caster (superfine) sugar
125 ml (4 fl oz) water
125 ml (4 fl oz) lemon juice
rind of 1 lemon, julienned

Preheat your oven to 180°C (350°F) and grease and line a 23 cm (9 in) spring-form cake tin.

To make the cake, combine the sugar and egg yolks in an electric mixer and beat until pale and creamy. Fold in the semolina, almond meal, salt, Cointreau, lemon juice and zest.

Whisk the egg whites to form stiff peaks. Gently fold them into the cake mixture. Pour into the cake tin and bake for 30 minutes or until cooked. Remove the cake from the oven and cool in the tin on a wire rack.

To make the ricotta filling, beat the ingredients together until smooth. Refrigerate until cold.

To make the syrup, combine the sugar, water, lemon juice and rind in a heavy-based saucepan. Heat gently to dissolve the sugar then increase the heat and bring to the boil. Simmer for 5 minutes to form a syrup then remove from the heat and leave to cool slightly.

When ready to assemble, split the cooled cake in half horizontally and spread the base with lemon curd. Spread with the chilled ricotta mixture then place the other half on top. Drizzle with the syrup and serve with Peaches Poached in Lemon Syrup (page 203).

Serves 10

....

Koulourakia

In Greece there seem to be as many versions of koulourakia as there are cooks. Everyone has their own particular way of making them. Koulourakia can be sweet, as in this recipe, or savoury, using feta or a hard cheese such as kephalograviera. They are quick and easy to make and can be formed into a variety of shapes. I like to roll them in sesame seeds and twist them.

500 g (1 lb 2 oz) plain (all-purpose) flour
1 teaspoon bicarbonate of soda (baking soda)
1 teaspoon ground cinnamon
½ teaspoon ground cloves
200 g (7 oz) caster (superfine) sugar

2 eggs, beaten
100 ml (3 ½ fl oz) corn oil
125 ml (4 fl oz) fresh orange juice
zest of 1 orange
100 g (3 ½ oz) sesame seeds

Preheat the oven to 180°C (350°F). Grease and line a baking tray.

Sift the flour, bicarbonate of soda, cinnamon and ground cloves together into a large mixing bowl. Stir in the sugar.

In another bowl, mix the eggs with the oil and orange juice and add the orange zest. Stir the egg mixture into with the flour and use your hands to shape it gently into a ball.

Break off walnut-sized pieces of dough and roll into thin sausages 10 cm long. Scatter the sesame seeds over the work surface and roll each little sausage in the seeds so it is evenly coated. Bend in half and twist to entwine. Arrange the koulourakia on the baking tray and bake for 30 minutes. Remove from the oven and cool on a wire rack. They will keep in an airtight container for up to a week.

Makes 25

Kourabiedes

These almond shortbread biscuits (cookies) are made at Christmas time in nearly every Greek home. They will usually be arranged on a plate in a pyramid shape and drenched in icing (confectioners') sugar – which looks very Christmassy, especially if the plate is wrapped in red cellophane paper. At A la Grecque we make them throughout the year as they are perfect to serve with a mid-morning coffee.

250 g (9 oz) unsalted butter
70 g (2 ½ oz) icing (confectioners') sugar, plus another 150 g (5½ oz) for dusting
1 egg yolk
1 teaspoon vanilla essence

1 tablespoon brandy
330 g (11 ½ oz) plain (all-purpose) flour
1 teaspoon baking powder
300 g (10½ oz) slivered almonds, lightly toasted

Preheat the oven to 180°C (350°F) and grease and line a baking tray.

Beat the butter in an electric mixer until pale and fluffy. Add 70 g (2 ½ oz) icing sugar and beat well. Add the egg yolk, vanilla and brandy and mix in well.

In another bowl, sift the flour with the baking powder then fold it into the butter mixture. Stir in the slivered almonds. The mixture will be quite stiff.

Flour your hands and break off spoonfuls of the dough. Roll into 6 cm (2½ in) sausages and form into crescent shapes, pinching the ends to a point. Arrange the kourabiedes on the baking tray and refrigerate for 10 minutes before baking.

Bake for 20 minutes until the biscuits are just beginning to colour a pale gold. Remove from the oven and dust generously with the remaining icing sugar while they are still warm. The biscuits should keep for up to a week.

Makes 25

Walnut biscotti

Biscotti are always useful to have on hand. They keep in an airtight container for a week or more (if you don't eat them all at once) and they are perfect with a mid-morning coffee.

I particularly like the combination of walnuts, brandy and spices in this recipe, but you can change the combination of nuts and spices to taste. For instance, pistachio nuts are good with fennel seeds or with a mixture of ground and crystallised ginger. Just make sure the pistachios are unsalted.

....

200 g (7 oz) butter
200 g (7 oz) caster (superfine) sugar
2 eggs
1 tablespoon brandy
1 teaspoon vanilla essence
440 g (15 ½ oz) plain (all-purpose) flour

1 teaspoon baking powder
1 teaspoon ground cinnamon
1 teaspoon ground nutmeg
200 g (7 oz) toasted walnuts, chopped
1 egg, beaten

Preheat the oven to 180°C (350°F) and grease and line a baking tray.

Beat the butter and sugar in an electric mixer until pale and fluffy. Add the eggs, one at a time, beating well after each addition. Stir in the brandy and vanilla.

In another bowl, sift the flour with the baking powder and spices then fold it into the egg mixture. Stir in the walnuts and form the dough into a round. Tip it out onto a floured work surface and knead briefly to form a ball. Divide into two even pieces and shape each into a 40 cm x 5 cm (16 in x 2 in) log.

Transfer the two logs onto the baking tray and brush each with a little beaten egg. Bake for 25 minutes then remove from the oven and cool on the tray.

When cool enough to handle, slice each log into 3 cm (1 ¼ in) slices on a diagonal. Arrange on the baking trays and return to the oven for 7–10 minutes until golden brown on both sides.

Cool the biscotti on a wire rack and store in an airtight container for 1–2 weeks.

Makes about 25

Eating the Greek way

For the best meals, you always need to begin with the best ingredients. This is particularly true of Greek food, which revolves around what is seasonally available. So don't waste your time making tomato soup in the winter, or looking for asparagus in the autumn. Cook broad (fava) beans in the spring and enjoy figs in the summer. If you're planning on making marmalade, do it in the winter when the oranges are in season, and make plum jam in February when they are plentiful.

Undoubtedly the freshest and tastiest produce will be what you grow yourself. Of course not everyone has the space, time or inclination to work a full garden to provide food for the table all year round — but nothing ever tastes as good as the produce you pick from your own garden, and prepare for the dinner table that evening. It is immensely satisfying to consume the fruits of your own labour, knowing that no pesticides or artificial fertilisers have been used and that the vegetables have not been transported long distances, handled by numerous people and held in cold storage or sat on a supermarket shelf before reaching your plate.

However, if you are headed to the market or the greengrocer to purchase fresh produce, it is helpful to have an idea of what to look for and what to be wary of. With vegetables, fruit and herbs, wherever possible, look at the stalk first. A fresh eggplant (aubergine) will have a lively green prickly stem; tomatoes and grapes should also have green healthy stems. A dry, brown or withered stalk or stem is a sure sign that the vegetable is not fresh. (The exceptions, of course, are pumpkins and onions, which are suited to drying and storing through the winter.) The flesh of all fruit and vegetables should be firm, shiny and of a good colour, not soft, wrinkled or bruised. Greens should look bright and lively, beans should be crisp and crunchy.

When buying fish, look for flesh that is firm, white or pink, not flaky or grey. The eyes of a whole fresh fish will be moist and raised, not sunken or dry. And fish should not smell 'fishy' or of ammonia.

Buying the best quality ingredients does not preclude buying cheaper cuts of meat or discarded pieces of fish. A dollar's worth of lamb's liver can feed a family of four, a couple of lamb necks will make a delicious soup and 1 kg (2 lb 3 oz) of stewing steak can become a warming wholesome stew. Heads and shells of prawns (shrimp) or crayfish can be turned into intensely flavoured bisques, and even a snapper's head which most people would toss in the bin, can be cooked on the barbecue and the sweet flesh picked out of the cavities to make a very satisfying meal.

The flavours and aromas of Greece are reflected in the products that we use at A la Grecque. The staple ingredient of the Mediterranean diet is undoubtedly olive oil, but along with olive oil, no Greek table is complete without tomatoes and feta cheese. Our gardens at Lorne and at our village house in Greece overflow with tomatoes throughout the summer and we eat them for breakfast, lunch and dinner in some form or other. While sun-ripened tomatoes, sweet from the vine, are a taste sensation on their own, if you sprinkle them with a little salt and freshly ground black pepper, drizzle on some olive oil and add a creamy piece of feta and a crust of bread, you have a most satisfying meal.

Feta is the most versatile of cheeses: it can be eaten hot or cold and it pairs with fruit, bread, pasta, rice, eggs, salads and vegetables. It can be crumbled onto soups, marinated and spiced with dukkah, pepper, basil or oregano, stuffed into capsicums (peppers) and baked. It marries perfectly with watermelon or rockmelon (canteloupe), but best of all, any time of the day, with tomato.

Finally, a brief word about presentation: in my view, nothing is more overwhelming than being presented with a great big plateful of food. I prefer to serve small portions, always taking care with the presentation to ensure there are no drops or splashes on the side of the plate. And I tend to avoid using garnishes, unless they are an integral part of the dish: keep it simple and let the food speak for itself.

The Greek pantry

Bakalao (salt cod) and Ranga (smoked and dried mackerel)

A mezze plate will always include some salty morsels to stimulate the appetite and assist in the appreciation of tsiporo or ouzo. Salted fish are common elements of a mezze plate, often in the form of anchovies, Chargrilled Sardines (page 106), Salt Cod Croquettes (page 50) or ranga, which is cooked over an open flame, then peeled and doused in Latholemono (page 160).

Bligouri

Bligouri is the Greek name for bulgur or cracked wheat. In Greece, village women make bligouri after the wheat has been harvested. First it is washed, then boiled in large cauldrons of water until it expands and softens. The cooked wheat is then spread out on sheets to dry in the sun. The outer husk is removed from the dried wheat and the grains are cracked in a special crusher. Bligouri is stored in a dry place for use during the winter months. It is used in many dishes, and is particularly good with chicken.

Caperi

Caperi are baby capers and they grow abundantly throughout most of the Greek islands. They are a staple in every Greek household where they are kept salted and pickled. In Australia caperi are generally sold packed in salt and they must be thoroughly rinsed in cold water and drained before use.

Cheese

Feta Probably the most famous Greek cheese, feta is an essential item on every Greek table. It is a soft, white cheese that is aged for at least three months and stored in brine. The Greeks have the exclusive naming rights to the name 'feta', through the PDO (Protected Designation of Origin) awarded by the European Court of Justice in 2002. It limits the term 'feta' to cheeses made exclusively of sheep's milk, (at least 70%), and goat's milk, (no more than 30%), in certain areas of Greece. The Commission decided that the biodiversity of the land, coupled with the special breeds of sheep and goat that provide milk, gives feta a specific aroma and flavour. At A la Grecque we use the Olympos brand, but Dodoni is also a very good feta and is widely available in Australian supermarkets. Always wash feta thoroughly under cold water to remove the salt before using.

Kephalograviera A hard cheese made from goat's or sheep's milk. Kephalograviera is used for grating and as a table cheese, and also for grilling (broiling) or frying, when it is referred to as 'saganaki'. The Greek islands of Naxos and Crete are particularly famous for their graviera cheeses, but here in Australia we use the Matis brand that comes from Trikala on the Greek mainland.

Kasseri A softer, milder cheese that is excellent for eating as a table cheese, but which is also good for melting in toasted sandwiches, pasta, pizza or rice.

Cream

Cream is not widely used in Greek cooking, but occasionally I will suggest that a cake or dessert be served with cream — especially poached quinces, which are particularly well suited to lashings of cream. When served as an accompaniment I always mean double or heavy cream. At A la Grecque we prefer to use King Island pure cream or Enterprize pure double cream (fat content 56%), but any fresh pure cream is fine.

When cooking with cream in a recipe I always use whipping cream, which has a 35% fat content. Whipping cream can be whipped, boiled or frozen.

Eggs

We only ever use free-range eggs, as we object to the cruelty of caging hens, the practice of de-beaking, the antibiotics and artificial diet they are fed, and the use of harsh lights to stimulate abnormal forced egg production. Chickens need exercise, fresh air and green grass. Free-range eggs have a natural colour, a better flavour and the whites hold better for poaching and whisking. At home we use eggs from our own hens and at A la Grecque we use locally produced eggs from the Otway Ranges.

Flower waters

Orange flower and rosewater are both used in Greek cooking to perfume desserts and sweets.

Garlic

Garlic is used in almost all savoury dishes. Good dry garlic should be pale and hard. Garlic which is yellowing may be flavourless and if it has a green shoot it may be bitter. Both should be discarded, or better still, planted in the garden to produce another plant. I plant garlic all year round and whenever I find a clove with a green shoot in the centre, I take it home and plant it somewhere in my vegetable garden.

Green garlic is an immature garlic plant and is used in many recipes that use spring vegetables. The head, which is under the ground, should be about 4 cm (1½ in) in diameter. When you cut it you will notice that the cloves have not developed separately and the skin covering the cloves is not dry and papery, but is still soft and moist. Green garlic tastes sweet and the whole plant – leaves, stem and head – are washed, chopped and added to the cooking pot.

Herbs

With a few exceptions, we use fresh herbs rather than dried, because they have a fresher flavour. Unless you dry them yourself, dried herbs can quickly deteriorate and become tasteless or, worse still, bitter. Fresh herbs are easily grown in pots or in the garden and are invaluable in everyday cooking, transforming a simple salad, a humble potato, soups, vegetable dishes, stews and grills.

Coriander Although not commonly used in Greek cooking, coriander is fairly widely available in Greece and I include it in some recipes. I like to use the fragrant ground seeds in Dukkah (page 36) and fresh coriander (cilantro) leaves in Chicken Breasts Roasted 'en Papillote' (page 150).

Dill Widely used in vegetable dishes and salads, dill is also perfect with mussels and in dressings to accompany fish. It is a major flavour component in Koukia (page 93) and Fricassee of Lamb and Spring Vegetables (page 43) and can be added to a simple lettuce salad with a squeeze of lemon juice for a surprising taste treat.

Mint Always used fresh, mint adds freshness and lifts the flavour of Keftethes (page 154), Tzatziki (page 47) and Fattoush (page 172).

Oregano The Greeks use a lot of dried oregano – *rigani* – in their everyday diet: on grilled (broiled) meats, in salads, in latholemono, and on a slice of feta. To avoid an unpleasant bitter flavour, use freshly dried oregano sparingly, and don't add it to the cooking pot. Instead, sprinkle a little on grilled meat or fried kalamari after cooking. The exception to this rule is Keftethes (page 154), where I do add a spoonful of dried oregano to the mix, but chopped fresh oregano would also work well.

Parsley An essential ingredient in Greek cooking. Use flat-leaf (Italian) parsley which has an excellent flavour. It is used fresh in salads, such as Konstantinopoli Salata (page 78) as well as a number of sauces and accompaniments. Parsley is also added to all manner of cooked dishes, such as soups, stews and braised vegetable dishes. Parsley is bi-annual and will self-seed and flourish in the garden if given plenty of moisture and some shade.

Honey

Greek honey has a stronger flavour than most Australian honeys. On the islands, the dried herbs of the rocky mountainsides – especially thyme – are the dominant flavours in the local honey. Used as a sweetener for desserts and pastries or simply drizzled over yoghurt, honey is a worthy inclusion in the pantry.

Kritharaki

A small rice-shaped pasta that is used in many Greek casseroles and soups. It is also sold in many supermarkets by the Italian name risoni or rosmarino. Kritharaki is usually cooked in the meat juices so that it absorbs the flavours of the dish. It is generally cooked until quite soft, instead of al dente.

Nuts, seeds and dried fruit

Use the freshest available as they will spoil if kept for long periods. Store walnuts in the fridge during the summer. Toast almonds, hazelnuts and walnuts lightly to enhance the flavour, then rub the skins away with a clean tea (dish) towel before using.

Olive oil

All of our salads, dressings, dips, vegetable dishes and sauces are made with cold-pressed extra virgin olive oil from Greece – preferably Sitia or Arcadia brand. I prefer green olive oils to yellow ones as I find they are slightly more tart, being made from less ripe fruit, and the flavour is nutty and fresh. Olive oil should be stored in a cool, dark place and should be used within twelve months of production. For frying, use a good quality vegetable oil such as corn or safflower.

Olives

An indispensable item in Greece, where many families – especially in rural areas – still preserve their own olives in salt or in brine. At A la Grecque we buy many different types of olives and use them mixed together and marinated as an appetiser, or separately in various dishes. Some of our favourite Greek olives are the firm black kalamata olives, cracked green olives, and small stuffed and jumbo golden olives. We also use large green olives from Spain and tiny wild Australian olives from South Australia. Wash olives before eating as they are often stored in brine.

Ouzo or tsiporo

Distilled from grapes, this is a clear spirit that is flavoured with aniseed and other herbs and spices. It is usually drunk at room temperature with ice or water, when it turns milky-white.

Pastourmas

Pastourmas is cured beef with a spicy paprika crust, and it is available from Greek or Turkish delicatessens. Pastourmas is usually sliced paper-thin and served on its own as a cold appetiser.

Pastry

Paper-thin filo pastry is used in Greek savoury and sweet pies. I like to make my own (page 190), or, if pressed for time, I purchase a handmade Turkish variety of filo, known as emek yufka for making Spanakotiropita (page 192), Pastourmopita (page 191), and for some desserts. Emek yufka is available in many Greek and Turkish supermarkets and is far superior to factory-made filo sheets which lack flavour and substance. Emek yufka can be frozen successfully.

Pomegranate molasses

A thick syrup made from boiled and concentrated pomegranate juice. Pomegranate molasses has a sweet–sour flavour and is used throughout the Middle East and in parts of the Eastern Mediterranean in dressings and salads.

Rice

A lot of rice is grown around Thessaloniki on the Greek mainland and Greek housewives will have any number of different types of rice in their pantry. The most common is golden rice (kitrino), which is used for pilaf; white, medium-grain rice for stuffed vegetables and Dolmades (page 54), and risotto (arborio) rice for Spanakoriso (page 170) and Prassoriso (page 168). The same varieties are available in Australia, but I also often use brown or wild rice for a different look and a very nutty flavour.

Semolina

Both fine and coarse semolina are used in Greek cooking, especially in desserts and in sweets such as Semolina Halvas (page 210). Both types have a great texture and because semolina is absorbent it teams very well with syrups.

Spices

For the best flavour, I recommend grinding spices as you need them. I sometimes use a mortar and pestle, but for larger quantities I use a small electric coffee grinder. Roast seeds such as cumin, coriander, fennel and white pepper in the oven for a few minutes until they are fragrant, then grind them and use as required. At the restaurant we grind black pepper every day.

Aniseed Perhaps best known as the dominant flavour of ouzo, aniseed is also used in some Greek biscuits (cookies) and cakes.

Cinnamon Frequently used in desserts, especially when sprinkled over halvas, rice pudding and syrupy cakes. Cinnamon quills are used to flavour the syrup used for baklava, and ground cinnamon is sprinkled onto the finished dish before serving. Cinnamon is also used in some meat dishes but I hardly ever use it, except for Chicken Breasts Roasted 'en Papillote' (page 150).

Cumin One of my favourite spices. Cumin can be quite dominating if used carelessly, but in the right place and in the right amount, it is exotic and evocative, vividly transporting you to spice markets in faraway places. Roast a handful of seeds and grind them whenever you need to add them to a dish. Make sure you only roast them for a minute or so until fragrant as they become unpleasantly bitter if overcooked.

Fennel Fennel seeds are used in some savoury cakes, such as Polenta Cake with Pine Nuts and Dried Fruit (page 234), and are toasted and ground for using in Dukkah (page 36), Sauce à la Grecque (page 162). In Greece, fennel seeds are often infused to make tea which is fed to babies with colic or served as a digestive for adults.

Mahlep The dried seeds of a variety of wild cherry tree, these are used as a flavouring in Eastern Mediterranean cooking – especially in festive breads and cakes, such as Tsoureki (page 188).

Masticha (mastic) The dried resin from an acacia tree, which is native to the island of Chios in the eastern Aegean Sea. Masticha is used to flavour sweets, ice creams, liqueurs and some breads and cakes. Its texture also makes it popular as a chewing gum and natural breath freshener and it is now widely available and very popular in cosmetics due to the brilliant marketing of the Masticha Farmers of Chios Cooperative.

Ras-el-hanout A combination of Middle Eastern spices, for which there is not just one recipe. It is a mix of 'top shelf' spices and flavours and can be made with any number of quantities or combinations according to your taste. Grind the spices individually and combine them to suit yourself. Add a little of the spice mix to a dressing of olive oil and vinegar to jazz up a salad or some chargrilled vegetables; rub some onto meat, fish or chicken before cooking; and try sprinkling a little onto roast pumpkin and potatoes.

Saffron Greek saffron is grown principally at Kroko near Kozani on the Greek mainland. Saffron is used in some Greek recipes to add colour and flavour. I particularly use it to flavour Saffron Pilaf (page 169) and dressings which accompany fish. Saffron can also be valuable in flavouring poached pears and custards.

Stock
At A la Grecque we make our own stocks from bones and vegetables. I have included recipes for basic stocks in the text (page 26–7).

Tahini
Paste made from ground sesame seeds, tahini is used to make hummus and some sauces, such as Parsley and Tahini Sauce (page 162). It can also be added to yoghurt and thinned out with a little lemon juice to make a very simple and interesting sauce. There are many brands available and I prefer to buy tahini from a health food shop.

Tarama
Tarama is traditionally made from grey mullet roe, but these days most commercial versions are made from other fish roe, such as cod or ling, and artificially coloured a brilliant pink. Tarama is very salty, so don't add any salt when making Taramosalata (page 48).

Vine leaves
In the Greek villages, fresh vine leaves are only gathered in the spring from nearby vineyards. The vines are pruned to leave only the branches bearing fruit. All other branches are removed, which allows all of the plant's energy and goodness to go into the fruit. The vine leaves are trimmed and blanched before using. They are perhaps most familiar as Dolmades (page 54), which are parcels stuffed with rice and herbs, or as Sarmathakia (page 55), parcels stuffed with rice and pork. These are both delicious and are often kept in the fridge to serve as a snack or as a mezze. Preserved vine leaves are often sold in jars in supermarkets and make an adequate alternative if fresh are not available. Wash them thoroughly before use as they are stored in brine.

Vinegar
We use red and white wine vinegar from Greece or Italy. Red wine vinegar is a little sweeter and more dominating, and matches the stronger flavours of octopus, roasted red capsicums (peppers) and rocket (arugula). White wine vinegar adjusts the sweetness of beetroot (beet), enhances the flavour of saffron and provides a balance to salted cucumbers.

Yoghurt
Enhances both sweet and savoury dishes. Yoghurt balances the sweetness of fruit compotes and jams, marries perfectly with lemon and counters strong, spicy flavours in meat, chicken or fish dishes. It adds a tang to fried foods such as whitebait, kalamari, zucchini (courgette) and eggplant (aubergine). It can be used in cakes, in sauces or dolloped on top of a beetroot (beet) salad, or a spicy couscous. At A la Grecque we use two types of yoghurt: for breakfast dishes we like Meredith sheep's milk yoghurt (which has a higher fat content and distinctive rich flavour) and for cooking, making labne, for salads or to top a vegetable dish we use a Greek yoghurt which is made from cow's milk and strained to be thicker. Yoghurt which is left out of the fridge will sour, but can still be used in savoury dips such as Tzatziki (page 47), with lots of garlic, salt and fresh dill.

Index

Acknowledgements

My thanks to Kosta, Strato, Alex and Dom for their patience and encouragement and to all my women friends in Polypetron for advice and assistance. Thanks to Stephen Roddy, Kish Atwell and Vic Patterson for help in the garden.

Special thanks to photographer Mark Roper, designer Gayna Murphy, Ellie Smith and Mary Small at Hardie Grant, Leesa O'Reilly and Lucy Rushbrooke. Without their valuable assistance I could never have made this dream come true.